Yale Studies in English
Richard S. Sylvester, Editor
Volume 168

THE OLD ENGLISH ADVENT

A Typological Commentary by Robert B. Burlin

Yale University Press   New Haven and London   1968

for John C. Pope

Ecce lingua Britanniae, quae nil aliud noverat quam barbarum frendere, jamdudum in divinis laudibus Hebraeum coepit Alleluia resonare.

Gregory the Great

Among the bequests of Bishop Leofric to the Cathedral Library of Exeter, there was one manuscript (the only one still in its keeping) which an early cataloguer described as · *I · mycel Englisc boc be gehwilcum þingum on leoðwisan geworht*. This "large English book on miscellaneous subjects, written in verse," is now considered the greatest extant anthology of Old English poetry. The *Exeter Book* or *Codex Exoniensis* contains, at present, 123 folios of the original poetic text. Although the works themselves are much older, the volume was probably transcribed during the second half of the tenth century. According to Robin Flower,[1] it is the product of a Western scriptorium and dates from "between 970 and 990 and rather early than late in that period." The manuscript is neither illustrated nor highly ornamented but is written in what Flower describes as "the noblest of Anglo-Saxon hands." "The script," he continues, "achieves a liturgical, almost monumental, effect by the stern character of its design and the exact regularity of its execution."

The volume, before it was bound together with eight leaves from another manuscript, had apparently been subjected to rather rough handling. One folio at least is missing, since the first gathering contains only seven instead of the usual eight, and there is a possibility that another entire gathering might have disappeared from the beginning of the book. The first folio (designated eighth in the present foliation)[2] has been scored over with knife strokes and badly stained with a liquid, probably spilled from the same vessel that has left a circular impression near the center of the leaf. This damage has caused some difficulty in reading the text, but modern

1. *The Exeter Book of Old English Poetry* (London, 1933), p. 83. This collotype facsimile of the MS has valuable introductory chapters by R. W. Chambers and Max Förster as well as Flower.

2. Of the unrelated leaves at the opening of the book, only seven are numbered; the first, containing a modern inscription, is not included in this foliation.

photographic processes have enabled the editors to decipher all but one or two verses of this part of the manuscript.[3]

The work inscribed on the leaves of this mistreated gathering (ff. 8a-14a) is the object of the present study. The beginning of the text is lost, but the subject of the remaining 439 verse-lines is the Advent, the first Coming of Christ. This poem is followed in the *Codex* by two others of a similar religious theme. The first of these is signed by the poet Cynewulf and is largely a paraphrase of a Gregorian homily on the Ascension; the second treats, in a highly rhetorical manner, the Last Judgment. These three poems have been traditionally grouped together, under the illusion that they formed an Old English Christian epic, and were called by the name of their protagonist, *Christ*. The authorship of the entire piece was then assigned to Cynewulf. Neither this attribution nor the "unity" of the *Christ* has, however, gone unchallenged. The scholarship on these two problems is voluminous and has, until recently, all but precluded any critical evaluation of the poems in their own right.

It is not the purpose of this study to revive that smoldering dispute. The three poems in question were undoubtedly placed together in this order because of their common theme and the chronological sequence, and probably by the anthologist responsible for the compiling of the *Exeter Book* at some earlier stage of its development. There is, however, little internal evidence which would lead one to believe that they were composed as an inseparable trio.[4] Nor is the Cynewulfian authorship currently accepted. In contrast to an evident stylistic resemblance among his signed works, these three poems exhibit notable differences. But these problems are of no particular relevance to a critique of the individual poems, and one may therefore set them aside and consider the first work, here called the *Advent,* as an independent unit.

Although the *Exeter Book* as a whole has been edited several times,[5] the *Advent* has been printed only once with full scholarly apparatus, in

3. See the "Transcription of the Damaged Passages of the Exeter Book" in the facsimile volume, pp. 68–82. For an ultraviolet reading of fol. 8, see Neil R. Ker, in *MÆ, 2* (1933), 225, and A. H. Smith, "The Photography of Manuscripts," *London Mediaeval Studies, 1* (1937–9), 179–207, esp. plate IX.

4. For a discussion of the MS evidence, see George Philip Krapp and Elliott Van Kirk Dobbie, eds., *The Exeter Book,* Anglo-Saxon Poetic Records, III (New York, 1936), pp. xxv–ix.

5. By Thorpe (1842), Grein (1857–58), Wülker (1881–98), Gollancz and Mackie (1895, 1934), and Krapp and Dobbie (1936).

the monumental edition of the *Christ* by Albert S. Cook.[6] While this work offers little in the way of critical evaluation, the research into the background and sources of the poems and the preparation of the text represent a distinguished achievement in Old English scholarship. More recently, Jackson J. Campbell has produced a text emphasizing the subdivisions of the poem, which he entitles *The Advent Lyrics of the Exeter Book,* [7] "edited alone and for themselves" for the first time. The aim of his book was to study the "lyrics" as "poems rather than as documents," and he therefore prefaces his collection of poems and translations with structural analyses of each unit. Campbell's edition has freed the poem from Cook's heavy apparatus and antiquated controversies, and increased its appeal to the modern student by his sensitive readings and an attractive presentation. His fragmentation of the sequence is, however, regrettable. My strategy has been to mediate between the historicism of Cook and the critical limitations of Campbell.

The key to our understanding of the Old English *Advent* is a peculiarly Christian set of mind, which I call the typological imagination. In my first chapter I have described the application of typology, first to scriptural exegesis and then to literary works of the Middle Ages. My concern is primarily for the formal implications of typological thinking, for the particular dimension conferred upon metaphor by the typologist's insistence on a historical continuum. This discussion is intended as a contribution to literary theory, not to theology or the history of biblical interpretation. I have tried to characterize the imaginative logic which underlies the exegetical procedures of even the most extravagant scriptural allegorist. But in any age religious belief and literary form are closely related; and the kind of imagination which was projected upon the Bible by its medieval interpreters can also be observed working in those poets who create new verbal structures for religious experience. I have illustrated the process here only by relatively uncomplicated examples of a traditional metaphor adapted to a new poetic context.

In the second chapter the imaginative structure of the *Advent* is considered in the light of recent critical estimates, the traditions of its antiphonal sources, and analogies to musical and modern poetic techniques.

---

6. *The Christ of Cynewulf* (Boston, 1900, rev. 1909), reproduced by Archon Books (Hamden, Conn., 1964) from the 1909 impression, with a new Preface by John C. Pope.

7. (Princeton, 1959). The quotations which follow are from p. vii of Campbell's Preface.

The commentary of the third chapter provides a thorough reconsideration of the liturgical sources and the patristic background of the typological figures in the *Advent,* as well as a detailed examination of specific textual problems. My chief aim, however, is to demonstrate the coherence of the poem as a whole, in terms of those metaphoric and temporal structures which characterize the typological imagination. I have prefixed the Old English text and a translation to each division of the commentary for convenient reference. My translation makes no claim to independent poetic value; it is merely intended as a handy gloss in a readable and reasonably modern idiom.

In conclusion, I would like to thank the Madge Miller Research Fund of Bryn Mawr College for assistance in the preparation of my manuscript, and Elizabeth Bogen, Rebecca Steinberg, and Sylvia Kartsonis for their labors at the typewriter, and Sheila Dickison and Professor Myra L. Uhlfelder for gracious help with the intricacies of Medieval Latin. I owe much to the many suggestions of the members of the Yale Studies in English Committee and their readers, and to the editors of the Press, particularly Mr. Wayland W. Schmitt. I am especially beholden to my colleague, Professor Isabel G. MacCaffrey, who worked patiently and valiantly with my text to make the rough places plain. My greatest debt, which extends far beyond instruction in Old English, is inadequately acknowledged in the dedication.

R.B.B.

Bryn Mawr
April, 1967

Contents

Abbreviations

*Es ist meine Überzeugung, dass
die typologische Exegese, so
wie sie von den grossen Predigern,
Exegeten und Hymnendichtern
verwendet wurde, mit ihrer
unendlichen Fülle von Kombinationen
und Anspielungen, Motivkreuzungen
und Metaphern, das eigentliche
Lebenselement der christlich
mittelalterlichen Dichtung bildet.*

Erich Auerbach

1. THE TYPOLOGICAL IMAGINATION

Genius in typology is the perception of affinities in Scripture, just as poetic genius is the perception of affinities in the natural world.

Jean Daniélou [1]

THE OPENING SENTENCE IN THE EXTANT FRAGMENT OF THE OLD English *Advent* tells us a good deal about the poem's imaginative assumptions:

Đu eart se weall-stan þe ða wyrhtan iu
wiðwurpon to weorce.

The metaphor, which offers a striking conjunction of divinity and architecture, is nevertheless set forth in the blandest of grammatical terms: "You [Christ] are the wall-stone which the workers of old rejected from the work." The simple copulative fixes a radical union which must either have been a familiar proposition or an extraordinary piece of poetic audacity. But the straightforward, earnest continuation of the metaphor in the lines which follow dispels any suggestion of mannered ingenuity. Of course, a source for these lines in the liturgy of the Advent season has made it clear that the image "lapis angularis" was in fact common property of the poet, his immediate audience, and all Latin Christendom. Indeed, the metaphoric tradition behind this passage may be said to have dominated the Christian imagination of the Middle Ages. A resource of abstruse theological meditation as well as more humble artistic work, such imagery, however, implied more than a habit of thought or a manner of speaking. It was a way of knowing, a confirmation of faith and community. Within and because of this tradition, the poet does, in fact, convey something of the triumphant astonishment inherent in the familiar terms. For him, though, the effect did not hang on a mere rhetorical device. Nor was the creative process to be equated with that poetic transmission of deep-felt emotion which we associate with a Romantic aesthetic. For the *Advent* poet the radical wonder of his image lay in the Incarnation itself, in that metaphysical revelation on which the metaphorical identity depends. The essential imaginative act occurred when the Word became flesh and dwelt among us. But since that Coming was for all time, though its manifestations

1. *Origen,* trans. Walter Mitchell (London, 1955), p. 257.

became ritualized and familiar, the inherent wonder remained, apparent to all men. Its recovery was available to each believer, while its recreation was the task of the poet.

Though the *Advent* poet's immediate inspiration was liturgical, it would be more accurate to describe his metaphoric domain as scriptural. What God expressed at the Incarnation, in terms of actual event, shed light on all other human happenings before and since, on the entire process of history from Creation to Judgment. The Bible is the verbal, temporal record of this divine expression of purpose, manifested in both word and event. For the medieval the Book itself had "something of the impersonal authority that we attach to a legal document. But it required no human seal of approval, for it was self-proclaiming, self-authenticating, unalterable by resolution, or change of human purpose or countermand." [2] The events, the language, and the images themselves which the religious poet chose to recreate derive from that authority, from the divinely imagined plan, of which he would have considered himself a humble, yet valued part.

Not only was the liturgy composed, to a great extent, of phrases and passages from the Bible, but the rituals of the Church were designed to recall and reenact the patterns of meaning which underlie all human happenings—the divine purpose which the Bible reveals within human history. The liturgy offers a ground plan of that vast construct of experience, while verbally it is an index of the written record. The *Advent* poet knew the seasonal antiphons not only in their particular context but also in relation to the liturgy as a whole and to the whole of the Bible, of which they are the abstract. He knew as well the commentaries of the Church Fathers, in which the meaning of Scripture and history was further explored, and some of which found their way into the liturgy itself. The poet's mind moved about freely in the wide concordance of scriptural forms and meanings. His imagination could associate words and events, disconnected in the text but related in ultimate significance. In the opening lines, for example, he gives us not only a paraphrase of the antiphonal phrase, "lapis angularis qui facis utraque unum," but a collocation of related images—a stone which the workers rejected, the house constructed by God and fallen into ruin, and a body which shared the same Creator and suffers a similar fate. The full import of these particular images will be discussed at a later time. What interests us here is the kind of mind that governed the structure of these details.

To understand the *Advent,* we must know something of the way in

2. Geoffrey Shepherd, "Scriptural Poetry," in *Continuations and Beginnings,* ed. E. G. Stanley (London, 1966), p. 1.

which the word of God in the Scriptures was understood by the medieval imagination. When we have looked at some of the characteristic forms of scriptural exegesis, we may have a better notion of the value that may be attached to scriptural images when they are incorporated into a literary work.[3] More important is the sense such an investigation may give us of the kinds of imagining that determine the structure of a poetry in an era which, as a condition of faith, looked beyond itself to a transcendent act of imagination—the continuing process of divine creation which underlies all human history and experience.

Within a Christian period every human act of creation must necessarily be considered a secondary or imitative one—hence, no doubt, the absence of a medieval poetic of any great significance. But since a verbal record for the archetype of creation is available in the Scriptures, the exegetical concept of the divine imagination may provide a valuable substitute for poetic theory. In the following pages I propose to cover what may be familiar ground to many, but I wish to consider not so much the terms or specific content of scriptural exegesis, as the range of imaginative forms which came to be included within a common understanding of the scriptural process. Once we have surveyed the gamut of biblical imagery and its interpretation, we can turn to literary recreations of these images to see how their accommodation to a new medium brings with it a corresponding sense of imaginative structure. In making these explorations, I shall range far beyond the specific scriptural content of the *Advent* and far beyond the Old English period for literary examples. My purpose is to lay bare a broad foundation on which rests not the *Advent* alone but much Christian religious poetry of the Middle Ages and later periods as well.

SCRIPTURAL TYPOLOGY

The governing principle common to all of the imaginative structures to be discussed is best described as typology. A good working definition of this much-debated term has been proposed by K. J. Woollcombe: "the establishment of historical connections between certain events, persons

3. Much recent debate in literary circles has centered on the issue of "Patristic Exegesis in the Criticism of Medieval Literature." Of some relevance to the present discussion are the papers of E. Talbot Donaldson, R. E. Kaske, and Charles Donahue, in Dorothy Bethurum, ed., *Critical Approaches to Medieval Literature,* Selected Papers from the English Institute, 1958–1959 (New York, 1960). The essay of Donahue is of particular interest on the question of the survival of historical typology in later medieval exegesis.

or things in the Old Testament and similar events, persons or things in the New Testament." [4] The operative word, "historical," precisely isolates what is most distinctly Christian about this tradition in medieval exegesis. The biblical interpretation of the early Fathers was heavily indebted to both Palestinian and Hellenistic techniques, but the typological perspective is essentially a product of Christian revelation. Though to some extent an outgrowth of Hebraic ideas of history and prophecy, the concept of the New Dispensation as a fulfillment of the Old forced a complete rupture. The Incarnation and the eschatological message of the Gospels marked an end to history and prophecy as the Jewish tradition had known them. The New Testament both concluded and absorbed the vision of the Old. The evangelization of the early Christians to the Jews sought to prove that the long debate between God and His chosen people had been resolved and that everything contained in sacred record pointed to this resolution.[5]

The new interpretation of history, which emerged in the exploration of the new faith, gave rise to the doctrine of the consonance or harmony of the two Testaments. As R. L. P. Milburn has written:

> the view gradually gained acceptance that, in the providential ordering of affairs by God, the events of the Old Testament were carefully designed to foreshadow and prepare the way for those redemptive actions which were to mark the decisive turning-point in the history of the world. St. Augustine expressed this belief by the formula: "In the Old Testament the New lies hid; in the New Testament the meaning of the Old becomes clear," while Paulinus of Nola put the matter thus in his poetic jingle:

4. "The Biblical Origins and Patristic Development of Typology," in *Essays in Typology,* Studies in Biblical Theology, No. 22 (London, 1957), p. 39. Much of the discussion which follows is indebted to Woollcombe's essay.

5. It is possible to speak of a typology within the Old Testament, as does A. C. Charity in his excellent study *Events and Their Afterlife* (Cambridge, 1966). Christian typology, however, is significantly different, and the contrast lies, it might be said, in the eschatology. For Man in Israel the "fulfilment of the way of Yahweh is never complete, but always in promise" (Charity, p. 59); the increase in the kingdom of Yahweh to include all men lies in the future. For the Christian this promise is fulfilled in the establishment of the Church of Christ on earth. The nature of that kingdom will be altered at the world's end, but only in its form or *figura.* (See Auerbach's statement, p. 7, below.) Hence the Christian has a point of typological reference not available to Israel, for whom all is prediction or expectation. Only with the Incarnation is the antitype genuinely a part of the historical process.

"The Old Law establishes the New, the New Law completes the Old. In the Old you find Hope, in the New, Faith. But the grace of Christ links Old and New Together." [6]

Not only were all Hebraic prophecies fulfilled with the coming of the true Messiah, but all historic events described in the Old Testament were also prophetic of the redemptive acts described in the New. The accord between the two Testaments was consequently of profound historical and doctrinal importance. While the explication of this accord was basically a theological activity, it offered the added homiletic value of dealing in concrete story and image. Typological exegesis, in fact, remained a respected exercise until very recent times, in spite of the temptation, which many medievals could not resist, to turn it into little more than an ingenious game.

Christian typology differs from other forms of exegesis known to the classical world, in its emphasis upon historical continuity.[7] The allegorical methods of Greek teachers and philosophers, Neoplatonist and Stoic alike, willingly discarded the text or image as of little importance once its spiritual meaning had been extracted. Historical typology, on the other hand, preserves the primary form or literal meaning along with the antitype which it prefigures. It reflects some of the fundamental tenets of Christian thought by the value it finds in matter, in process, and in the human person. Just as the crucified Lord harrowed the bodies as well as the souls of the Patriarchs and Prophets out of hell, so the Christian typologist accords the Old Testament figures a value and reality as historical entities after their spiritual mission has been fulfilled. Once their

6. *Early Christian Interpretations of History* (London, 1954), p. 107. The statement of Augustine is from the *Comm. in Exod.* 73, and the poem of Paulinus is in *Ep.* xxxii. 5:

> Lex antiqua novam firmat, veteram nova complet:
> In veteri spes est, in novitate fides,
> Sed vetus atque novum coniungit gratia Christi.

7. Charity, in *Events and Their Afterlife,* gives the best explanation, known to me, for the necessity of a historical continuum in true typology, which he sees as an "existential confrontation between man and the action of God" (p. 159). Though he would doubtless disallow many of the examples cited in this chapter, the sense he gives of the psychological and ethical rationale of typology is of great importance and central to my argument. Charity's objections to patristic exegesis (pp. 161–64), with its neglect of historical action, I shall attempt to minimize in the following pages, but they are best answered in the literary works I discuss, which do in fact incorporate that essence of what he sees as true scriptural typology.

function as heralds and types of the Redeemer has been acknowledged, they still retain a place in the continuum of human experience and are not to be cast off as empty husks or the mere illusion of an evanescent world.

The relationship of history to spirit in typological thinking is brilliantly analysed by Erich Auerbach in his essay on the word, "Figura." As a romance philologist, he naturally prefers the Latin rhetorical term to the more theological Greek "typos," but his definition is central to this discussion:

> Figural interpretation establishes a connection between two events or persons, the first of which signifies not only itself but also the second, while the second encompasses or fulfills the first. The two poles of the figure are separate in time, but both, being real events or figures, are within time, within the stream of historical life. Only the understanding of the two persons or events is a spiritual act, but this spiritual act deals with concrete events whether past, present, or future, and not with concepts or abstractions; these are quite secondary, since promise and fulfillment are real historical events, which have either happened in the incarnation of the Word, or will happen in the second coming. Of course purely spiritual elements enter into the conceptions of the ultimate fulfillment, since "my kingdom is not of this world"; yet it will be a real kingdom, not an immaterial abstraction; only the *figura,* not the *natura* of this world will pass away, and the flesh will rise again.[8]

When St. Paul refers to Adam as "a foreshadowing [*typos*] of him that was to come" (Rom. 5:14; "forma futuri" in the Vulgate), he has in mind a "pattern or model for Christ."[9] The "type" looks toward the incarnate Christ, the "Second Adam," Who within history reverses the

8. In *Scenes from the Drama of European Literature* (New York, 1959), pp. 53–54. This essay was translated by Ralph Manheim from the German text in *Neue Dante Studien* (Istanbul, 1944). Auerbach's later essay, *Typologische Motive in der mittelalterlichen Literatur,* Schriften und Vorträge des Petrarca-Instituts Köln, II (Krefeld, 1953), is also of some interest to the student of literary typology. He finds figural motifs in such generically different works as the *Song of Roland* and Dante's *Comedy,* which he distinguishes from the pure allegories of Alanus de Insulis. In his terms there would be no question of calling the *Advent* allegorical.

9. Woollcombe, *Essays in Typology,* p. 65. For an extended analysis of New Testament usage, see Woollcombe, pp. 60 ff., and John Wilkinson, *Interpretation and Community* (London, 1963), pp. 96 ff.

"form" of Adam's behavior. The relation of type and antitype depends upon the recurrence of the structure of event within the process of human experience. At the core of New Testament typology is a concept of historical recapitulation which Woollcombe has compared to the figure on a carpet:

> All the parts of the pattern were closely related to each other and converged on the central motif: and the pattern between the beginning and the central axis mirrored the pattern from the central axis to the end. Consequently the main object of their [the New Testament writers'] exegesis was to show how the parts of the pattern were related, and how they converged on the centre—to bring to light the evidence of God's consistent purpose in history.[10]

Historical reiteration and the fulfillment of prophecy, anticipated in the Old Testament and concluded in the New, became the basis of much patristic interpretation. Formulation of the theory is usually attributed to Irenaeus in the second century, and in his *Discourse in Demonstration of the Apostolic Preaching* he documented the idea of recapitulation with an astonishing abundance of detail. Here, for example, is only part of his expansion of the Pauline type of the "Second Adam":

> From this [the earth], then, whilst it was still virgin, God took dust of the earth and formed the man, the beginning of mankind. So then the Lord, summing up afresh this man, took the same dispensation of entry into flesh, being born from the Virgin by the Will and the Wisdom of God; that He also should show forth the likeness of Adam's entry into flesh, and there should be that which was written in the beginning, "man after the image and likeness of God" [Gen: 1:26].
>
> And just as through a disobedient virgin man was stricken down and fell into death, so through the Virgin who was obedient to the Word of God man was reanimated and received life. For the Lord came to seek again the sheep that was lost; and man it was that was lost: and for this cause there was not made some other formation, but in that same which had its descent from Adam He preserved the likeness of the (first) formation. For it was necessary that Adam should be summed up in Christ, that mortality might be swallowed up and overwhelmed by immortality; and Eve summed up in Mary, that a virgin should be a virgin's intercessor, and by a virgin's obedience undo and put away the disobedience of a virgin.

10. Woollcombe, *Essays in Typology,* p. 68.

And the trespass which came by the tree was undone by the tree of obedience, when, hearkening unto God, the Son of man was nailed to the tree; thereby putting away the knowledge of evil and bringing in and establishing the knowledge of good.[11]

These typological patterns go hand in hand with the theological justification of the Atonement and, as such, are repeated and expanded in learned discourse and popular art throughout the Middle Ages.

Irenaeus himself describes the process of recapitulation in terms of the tying and unloosing of a knot: "In no other way can that which is knotted be undone, but by bending the loops of the knot in a reverse order." [12] Historical typology, as the image suggests, has two basic requirements: that there be formal congruence in the repeated events, and that they be part of the same continuous process. Though these requirements, with some modification, are constants in Christian exegesis, they were threatened from the earliest times. The historicity of the Old Testament was all but ignored by the Alexandrian school of allegorists, and Augustine (XXXVIII.30–31) [13] would seem to have detected similar tendencies in his flock when he admonished them:

in the name of God to believe before all things when you hear the Scriptures read that the events really took place as is said in the book. Do not destroy the historic foundation of Scripture, without it you will build in the air. Abraham really lived and he really had a son by Sarah his wife . . . But God made of these men heralds of His Son who was to come. This is why in all that they said and in all that they did, the Christ may be sought and the Christ may be found. All that the Scriptures say of Abraham really happened, but he is at the same time a prophetic type.

The literal, historical sense of the Bible was the particular concern of the Antiochene exegetes, but they seem also to have worried about our first requirement and insisted upon an apparent formal kinship between type

11. St. Irenaeus, *The Demonstration of the Apostolic Preaching,* trans. J. Armitage Robinson (London, 1920), pp. 99–100. See also his *Against Heresies,* trans. John Keble (London, 1872), esp. Bk. III, chap. 22.

12. *Against Heresies,* Bk. III, p. 296.

13. All patristic references, so indicated, are to the *Patrologia latina* ed. J.-P. Migne, (221 vols. Paris, 1844–64) which is cited throughout for convenience of reference. Translations are my own, unless otherwise indicated. This translation is by Dora Nussey, in Emile Mâle, *Religious Art in France, XIII Century* (New York, 1913), pp. 135–36.

and antitype. Woollcombe (p. 73) cites as characteristic the statement of
Theodore of Mopsuestia: "It is surely obvious that every type has some
resemblance to that which it is said to typify." But it is precisely here that
typology came to admit considerable latitude. As long as the type was
drawn from Scripture, there could be a justifiable claim to historicity. But
the demand for a congruence of complex events—a sine qua non of modern apologists for typology—was weakened by the acceptance of accidental
details as typologically significant.

Even in the New Testament, ingenuity occasionally extended the bounds
of strict typological verisimilitude. The author of the Epistle to the Hebrews, for example, argues at length for the appropriateness of Melchisedech as a type of Christ. The figure, though casually introduced, is of
some importance to the *Advent* sequence. Let us look first at the poet's
method. Here the point of typological contact is Melchisedech's role as
lawgiver and teacher, but the passage is even more concerned with the
typological process itself. The lines in question follow immediately upon
the interpretation of the name Emmanuel:

> Swa þæt gomele gefyrn
> ealra cyninga cyning   ond þone clænan eac
> sacerd soðlice   sægdon toweard,
> swa se mære iu   Melchisedech,
> gleaw in gæste,   godþrym onwrah
> eces alwaldan.   Se wæs æ bringend,
> lara lædend,   þam longe his
> hyhtan hidercyme,   swa him gehaten wæs . . . (135b–42)

> [As sages of former times accurately foretold
> The King of all kings and immaculate Priest,
> So, too, of old the great Melchisedech,
> Wise in spirit, revealed the divine majesty
> Of the eternal Ruler.   He was the bringer of laws,
> The guide of learning to those who long
> Hoped for His coming, as it was promised them . . .]

The *swa. . . , swa . . .* construction suggests that the exemplary activity
of Melchisedech is exactly parallel to the speech of the prophets. Each in
its own medium—word or action—expresses a historical reality which is
only fully understood as revealed in the Incarnation. The subject of the
following sentence (*Se*, 140), with its ambiguous antecedent, rather strikingly implies the typological identity of Melchisedech and Christ. Both are
"bringers of laws" and "guides of learning," but only with the modifying

clause, "for those who long hoped for His advent," do we realize that the subject has become Christ exclusively. The grammar and syntax of this passage show how subtly and instinctively the *Advent* poet responded to the typological process.

The figure of Melchisedech is firmly rooted in Old Testament history, and there is no question of his authenticity on this count. But his typological relevance has been repeatedly questioned by modern theologians.[14] The author of Hebrews, we are told, "filled out his argument by making use of a rather dubious etymological link and some forced analogies." It was this kind of performance, stamped for the medieval with the authority of St. Paul, which sanctioned not only the corroboratory expansions, like those cited below, but also the sophistic imitations found in the best of medieval commentators. Accidental details were substituted for that formal congruence in repeated event which is essential to true typology. Yet Melchisedech, according to one rigorous student of the subject, does satisfy that requirement. The parallel, A. C. Charity maintains,[15] is established "from the point of view of vocation, and action in response to vocation. . . . The writer never loses sight of the main point of his prooftext [Psalm 109:4], the supreme High-priesthood of both 'type' and 'antitype.' " It is worth noting that for the *Advent* poet, too, the significance of this figure lies in his vocation, and the poet's sense of what is typologically valid seems in accord here with at least one modern view. But since the confusion of substance and accident in figural reference is responsible for much of the extravagance in later medieval exegesis, it will be valuable to examine the details of this particular case and follow their echoes among the commentators.

Melchisedech is a minor figure in the Book of Genesis (14:18–20), whose name recurs somewhat enigmatically in the Messianic Psalm (109:4): "Thou art a priest for ever according to the order of Melchisedech." The Epistle to the Hebrews (7:1–17) relates this prophetic text and the concept of the Hebraic priesthood in general to Christ. The association is made on four counts: his name, his origin, his sacerdotal order, and his superiority to Abraham. His name was etymologized as "king of justice"; and his title, "king of Salem," could be further interpreted as "king of peace" (Heb. 7:2). "Who other can this 'king of justice or peace' be," demands Alcuin (C. 1063) centuries later, "than our Lord Jesus

14. See, for example, G. W. H. Lampe, "The Reasonableness of Typology," in *Essays in Typology* (London, 1957), pp. 34–35.

15. All quotations in this paragraph are from his *Events and Their Afterlife,* p. 112.

Christ? For He made us just, bringing peace to everything which is in heaven and on earth. He alone is King of justice and peace."

The origin of Melchisedech is one of the mysteries of the Old Testament. Silence, where lengthy genealogies were common, led "Paul" to declare that Melchisedech was without ancestry, "having neither beginning of days nor end of life" (Heb. 7:3). This enigma prompted early commentators (including Augustine, XXXIV.567) to associate him with an angel or with the Holy Spirit, though Jerome (XXII.676–77) firmly insisted on the Talmudic explanation that he was Shem, son of Noah. But Ambrose (XVI.404) was among the first to note the possible typological ramifications of the New Testament text: "Without a mother according to His divine nature; because He was begotten of God the Father: without a father according to His incarnation, because He was born of a virgin: having neither beginning nor end, because He Himself is beginning and end of all, the first and the last."

Melchisedech is considered superior to Abraham, for he received tithes from the Patriarch and blessed him and, through Abraham, all the tribe of Levi, and "without any contradiction, the lesser is blessed by the better" (Heb. 7:7). Since Melchisedech was uncircumcised, the incident became in patristic exegesis a prefiguration of the uniting of the Jews and the Gentiles in one Church through the agency of Christ. Abraham recognized, according to Isidore (LXXXIII.240), "a future priesthood among the Gentile peoples, spiritually superior to that of the Levites, which was to be born from him in Israel, so that the uncircumcised priesthood of the Church would bless, in the circumcised Abraham, the priesthood of the Synagogue."

The superiority of the priesthood of Melchisedech is established by a "far-fetched process of reasoning" [16] according to which the Levitical tradition was attached to Moses and the Old Law, which brought nothing to perfection and was rejected with the Advent of Christ. So, too, the old priesthood was replaced by the new order of Him "Who is made, not according to the law of a carnal commandment, but according to the power of an indissoluble life" (Heb. 7:16). This was the "order of Melchisedech," spoken of in the prophetic Psalm, and stemming, like Christ, from the tribe of Judah.

Such typological embroidery, though based in the New Testament and related to the historical development in the Old, is, to some minds, unreal and irrelevant to Christian doctrine in general; it serves only as a con-

16. Lampe, *Essays in Typology,* p. 34.

venient apology suitable to the specific occasion, an *argumentum ad hominem*. "There is no clear correspondence between the type and the fulfilment, and no genuine historical recapitulation of a single pattern of the divine activity." [17] Yet such discrimination among Old Testament types was not common in medieval commentary. The Melchisedech analogy was relished for all its ingenious scriptural complexity and still further elaborated. The fact that he appeared to Abraham "bringing forth bread and wine" (Gen. 14:18) was taken as the most significant distinction between the two priesthoods. The new rite was accomplished, in the words of Jerome (XXIII.1011), "not through Aaron by the slaughter of unreasoning victims, but by the offering of bread and wine; that is, by the body and blood of the Lord Jesus." For Ambrose (XIV.427) this eucharistic typology conclusively identified Melchisedech with Christ, "Son of God, Priest of the Father, Who by the sacrifice of His body propitiated the Father for our sins."

The Milanese Doctor spoke for many centuries of future explicators when he concluded, in the *De fide* (XVI.607–08):

> Therefore we have taken this Melchisedech as a priest of God in the type of Christ; but the former as a type, the latter as the reality; for a type is the shadow of the reality [*typus autem umbra est veritatis*]; the former, a king in the name of one city, the latter a King in the reconciliation of the whole world.

The figure of Melchisedech,[18] so casually appropriated by the *Advent* poet, had a significance in the history of biblical interpretation which would be difficult to underestimate. With the sanction of New Testament procedure, the early Fathers pushed to extreme limits the possibilities of typological relevance. Extending in various and ingenious ways the connections with the antitype, they made of the great priest not only a type of Christ but an exemplary instance of the typological method itself. The *Advent* poet captures in his brief allusion this dual significance and so not only testifies to the vast importance Melchisedech had acquired for all Christians during the first millennium but confirms our sense of the ingrained habits of typological imagining in the poet himself.

17. Ibid.

18. For an exhaustive study of the exegetical history, see Gottfried Wuttke, *Melchisedech der Priesterkönig von Salem*, Beihefte zur Zeitschrift für neutestamentliche Wissenschaft und die Kunde der älteren Kirche, V, (Giessen, 1927).

Unacceptable though it may be to some theologians, the Melchisedech figure illustrates perfectly how far the medieval exegete was willing to extend the limits of typological linking, while retaining the essential requirement of historicity. Other extensions, however, entail a reinterpretation of the meaning of history. When the antitype is the incarnate Christ, as it is predominantly in the Synoptic Gospels, the scope of historical reference can be conventionally defined. But the work of Christ reaches, of course, beyond His earthly career; His participation in the Church and its sacraments and in the activity of the individual Christian soul has a greater, one might say "metahistorical" pertinence. The enlargement of the typological system to include such antitypes as these—temporal, yet encompassing all Christian history, ecclesiastical as well as personal—is the next step in our survey of the medieval view of the scriptural imagination.

The search for prefiguration of the sacraments of the Church was encouraged by passages in the fourth Gospel and in some of the Apostolic Epistles. Figures for baptism and the eucharistic sacrifice became a recognized part of the process of concordance, as, for example, when the First Epistle of Peter explains the "Ark of Noah," in which only eight souls were saved by water, as "baptism which, being of like form [*similis formae*], now saves you also . . . through the resurrection of Jesus Christ" (3:21). This slight reference to the familiar story of the Flood was then seized upon and diligently amplified in patristic times by the incorporation of further details from the Genesis account.[19] The following passage from the *De baptismo* of Tertullian (I.1209) is characteristic of early exegesis:

> Even as, after the waters of the flood, by which former sins were cleansed, after the "Baptism of the world," the dove, a herald sent from the ark, announced the appeasement on earth of heavenly wrath and brought back an olive branch, a sign which even among the gentiles is extended in peace; so, by a similar deployment of spiritual effects, the dove of the Holy Spirit flies down to the earth, that is, to our flesh emerging from the baptismal font after [the purgation of] former sins, and brings the peace of God, sent from the heavens, where the Church is the prefigured ark.

This ecclesiastical typology survives even in the unallegorical Antiochene tradition, probably because the sacrament can be associated with the

19. For a detailed examination of the figure, see Jean Daniélou, *Sacramentum futuri* (Paris, 1950), Bk. II; Eng. trans. Dom Wulstan Hibberd, *From Shadows to Reality* (Westminster, Md., 1960). See also Per I. Lundberg, *La Typologie baptismale dans l'ancienne Église* (Leipzig, 1942).

specifically historical: Christ is seen as a "New Noah," and the Flood is taken as a type of the Baptism of Christ. The unifying sign is the return of the dove to Noah, recapitulated in the descent of the Paraclete at the Baptism of Christ and figuring the presence of the Holy Spirit in the sacrament administered to all Christians by the Church.

From sacramental typology it is but a short step to what in allegorical terms is the tropological sense. The antitype is the individual Christian soul. Although the pattern was predominantly moral, in some hands, notably the Alexandrians', it was given a mystical turn.[20] A particularly useful illustration is the rich typology of Exodus. The historical type is alluded to repeatedly in the Gospel of Matthew; the life of Christ is presented as a fulfillment of the Old Testament prophecy of a New Exodus to be accomplished in the coming of the Messiah.[21] But in John and especially in the Epistles, the allusions are frequently given a sacramental gloss:

> You should understand, my brothers, that our forefathers were all under the [pillar of] cloud, and all passed through the [Red] Sea; and all were baptized into [the fellowship of] Moses, in the cloud, and in the sea: And they all ate the same spiritual food, and all drank the same spiritual drink; (they drank of the spiritual rock that followed them, and the rock was Christ). But with most of them God was not well pleased, for they were overthrown in the desert. Now these things were done in a figure [*in figura (typoi)*] of us, that we should not covet evil things as they also coveted. (I Cor. 10:1–6)

The last lines stress the moral or tropological application of the figure, but the Fathers found a rich mine in the sacramental analogy. Augustine explicates these lines of St. Paul in the *Contra Faustum* (XLII.269–70), the twelfth book of which is a compendium of Old Testament types and a justification of the method. The following excerpt shows something of the process of thought which this most influential of the Doctors of the Church imprinted upon biblical exegesis. It is not he but the Apostle who explicates in a typological fashion the flight from Egypt:

> By explaining one point, he has given the mind a key to the rest. For if Christ is the rock because of its firmness, why is Christ not also the

20. Henri de Lubac, *Exégèse médiévale* (4 vols. Paris, 1959–64), Pt. I, chap. 9, makes a useful distinction between what he calls "mystical tropology" and the anagogical or mystical sense of the fourfold allegorical method. The first seeks its "tenor" in the Way in which the soul approaches God, the second in a vision of the Goal itself, "what is to come."

21. See Daniélou, *Sacramentum*, pp. 131 ff.; trans. Hibberd, pp. 153 ff.

manna, the living bread which came down from heaven and gives spiritual life to those who partake of it? The Israelites, because they accepted the figure only in the carnal sense, are dead. But when the Apostle says, "They ate the same spiritual food," he demonstrates that this is also to be understood in a spiritual sense as Christ; just as he made clear why he had called the "drink" "spiritual," when he added that Christ was the rock. When this was made clear, all things became transparent. Why, then, is Christ not both the clouds and the pillar, for he is upright and firm and a support to our weakness: shining by night and not by day; so that those who do not see, may see; and those who see, may become blind? The clouds and the Red Sea are a baptism especially consecrated by the blood of Christ. The enemies following in the rear, like our past sins, perish. The people are led through the desert: so all those who have been baptized do not yet fully enjoy the promised land; because they do not see, hoping and waiting patiently, they are as it were in the desert.

The Israelites who passed through the Red Sea were the baptized, the types of those who composed the living Church of Christ, liberated from the power of the forces of evil. The Exodus, then, was a splendid vehicle for the progress of the individual Christian soul, sustained by the sacraments and supported by the Holy Spirit,[22] across the wilderness of terrestrial existence to the Promised Land.

But to the Christian Platonists of Alexandria the story of the Exodus contained a meaning for the soul, which departed so fundamentally from the typological tradition that Origen in his homilies was obliged to carry the two senses simultaneously. Alexandrian exegesis looks back to Philo, who explicated the life of Moses as an allegory of his spiritual theology.[23] The crossing of the desert became the progress of the soul divesting itself of the passions and moving toward the illumination of the "Logos." Father Daniélou, in *Sacramentum futuri,* demonstrates how Origen, in his

22. Some indication of how commonplace this piece of typology became is apparent in the casual allusion in the Old English *Exodus:*

> Him beforan foran   fyr and wolcen
> in beorhtrodor,   beamas twegen,
> þara æghwæðer   efngedælde
> heahþegnunga   Haliges Gastes
> deormodra siþ   dagum and nihtum.   (93–97)

23. See Erwin R. Goodenough, *By Light Light: The Mystic Gospel of Hellenistic Judaism* (New Haven, 1935), chap. 8: "The Mystic Moses," pp. 199 ff.

homilies on Numbers and Exodus, applies this allegory to the Christian "Word" of St. John's Preface and unites it with his version of historical typology:

> The departure from Egypt is a departure from the world. The three days of the journey are the purifying of words, deeds, and thoughts, or the three days which Christ spent in the tomb. Origen calls the first sense moral, the second mystical: he is simply putting side by side the influence deriving from Philo with that deriving from the catechetical instruction. Similarly, Moses praying with out-stretched arms signifies either the lifting of the mind above earthly things, or salvation through Christ's Cross, or the spiritual interpretation of the Law.[24]

Daniélou, whose exegetical views are more tolerant than those of some modern theologians, concludes that the figure of the progress of the Christian soul toward God is a legitimate interiorization of the Scripture: "Whether it is a nation or a single soul, it is the same God who leads them by the same ways." [25] But in the details he admits a distinction between the "legitimate extension of the literal sense" and others "purely allegorical." It is clear that we have come a long way from the strict concept of typology and have acquired a broad spectrum of interpretative possibilities, including the notion that a scriptural type is less apparently a historical event than a "quasi-sacramental presentation of spiritual reality in an outward and earthly form." [26]

Though there was considerable debate in the early Church between the literalist Antiochenes and those who would permit the discarding of the outer husk to find the kernel of inner spiritual meaning, the distinctions became less significant to later apologists and homilists. By the end of the first Christian millennium, collections of scriptural types had appeared which were both exhaustive and indiscriminate. There were catalogues, like the *Allegoriae* of Rabanus Maurus and the later *Glossa ordinaria,* which sought to identify every person, place, and object of biblical record, by providing an appropriate "inner" meaning or meanings. The personal types they used were based primarily on correspondence in action and event: Old Testament prefigurations of Christ, the Church, the sacraments, or the Christian soul, which we have discussed, and New Testament an-

---

24. *Sacramentum,* pp. 195–96; trans. Hibberd, pp. 221–22. For a substantial summary of Origen's spiritual exegesis of Exodus, see Daniélou, *Origen,* pp. 196 ff.

25. *Sacramentum,* p. 200; trans. Hibberd, p. 226.

26. Lampe, *Essays in Typology,* p. 30.

ticipations of the celestial Kingdom of the future—a final anagogical development for which Origen again is responsible.[27] No matter how "allegorical" or accidental the figural base, however, the understanding prevailed that type and antitype shared a common historical continuum in time and space. A scriptural typologist, such as the *Advent* poet, did not need to seek his images in the Book of Nature as did the authors of bestiaries and lapidaries, and the Book of the Word of God contributes a temporal dimension which encourages such historical justification. But it will be useful, in concluding this survey, to discuss some of the "catalogue" types, those dependent on a single word—a proper or common noun—and most distant from the concept of typology which emphasizes process or event. The *Advent* poet makes no distinction among his images, bringing "historical type" and "allegory" together in a single imaginative continuum.

A biblical personage might achieve typicality, or at least have it confirmed, by virtue of his name alone. We have already mentioned the etymologies of Melchisedech and Salem (above, p. 11). The delight in exploring the origins of personal and place names is common to both the Hebraic and Hellenistic [28] traditions. The name Joshua, "who was great according to his name" (Ecclus. 46:1), was interpreted as "savior" long before Christian exegesis identified him with Jesus. The name Emmanuel, though of Old Testament origin (Isa. 7:14), is first interpreted scripturally in Matthew (1:23) as "Nobiscum Deus." The etymology then became a vehicle for the doctrine of the two natures of Christ: "For He Who is God, born of the Father before all time, He Himself in the fullness of time became Emmanuel, that is, God-with-us, in the womb of His Mother, because He deemed it worthy to take on the frailty of our nature in the unity of His own person, when 'the Word was made flesh and dwelt among us' " (Rabanus, CVII.752–53).

In the study of proper names theology and not philology was the relevant discipline, and Christian explicators, like their Stoic predecessors,[29] were often satisfied with the vaguest resemblances. Such influential etymologists as Augustine and later the notorious Isidore of Seville were merely following a tradition of the antique world, in which the "invention" of word origins was an erudite game rather than a scientific pursuit. According to H.-I. Marrou, "it was above all a matter of making clear the 'true'

27. Daniélou, *Origen*, pp. 170 ff.
28. See Woollcombe, *Essays in Typology*, pp. 50–51.
29. See Wilkinson, *Interpretation and Community*, pp. 70–71.

sense of a term by an ingenious association." [30] Since the "true" sense was a matter of faith, it was often possible to find many links between the proper name and appropriate common "antecedents." Everyone is familiar with the five etymologies for the name Cecilie which Chaucer borrowed from the *Legenda aurea* in his Prologue to the *Second Nun's Tale*.[31] Chaucer was, of course, too sensitive to the history of languages to pass on this information for its philological value. He no doubt saw it, as did most medievals, as a convenient way of conveying something of the spiritual character, the "true sense," of the saintly person who bore the name. In any case, this sort of etymologizing had long since increased enormously the typological catalogues of persons and places.

The typologizing of scriptural objects, animate or inanimate, was at first a consequence of the historical event to which they were attached, as in the case of the bread and wine of Melchisedech. But they were soon investigated independent of the demands of their contexts. This process is best exemplified in the Marian figures, of which little has been said thus far. The comparatively slight role played by the Blessed Virgin in the Gospels required great ingenuity from her apologists if they were to substantiate her theological importance with Old Testament analogies. Types for Christ, such as Adam, could be duplicated, as we have seen in the instance of the "Second Eve," whose Latin name the angelic salutation, "Ave," reversed. Other matriarchs—Rachel, Esther, Judith—were occasionally exploited, but it was predominantly in symbolic objects that the popular types were found. These may be arbitrarily collected under three categories—the prophetic, the miraculous, and the allegorical—in a sequence which somewhat recapitulates the accretion of figures for Christ.[32]

In the Messianic prophecies which look toward the birth of the Savior, the Virgin might be expected to find a place. Isaiah, who explicitly declared, "Behold a virgin shall conceive, and bear a son" (7:14), later

---

30. Henri-Irénée Marrou, *Saint Augustin et la fin de la culture antique* (Paris, 1938), p. 128. See also Beryl Smalley, *The Study of the Bible in the Middle Ages* (Oxford, 1952), pp. 6, 8, and Ernst Robert Curtius, *European Literature and the Latin Middle Ages,* trans. Willard R. Trask (New York, 1953), pp. 495–500.

31. *The Works of Geoffrey Chaucer*, ed. F. N. Robinson, (2d ed. Cambridge, Mass., 1957), p. 208.

32. Many of the Marian figures discussed here are taken from the convenient list of Honorius of Autun in his chapter on the Annunciation in the *Speculum ecclesiae* (CLXXII. 904).

prophesied: "And there shall come forth a rod [*virga*] out of the root of Jesse, and a flower shall rise up out of his root. And the spirit of the Lord shall rest upon him" (11:1–2). The jingle of *"virgo-virga"* made the "rod or sprout of Jesse" an attractive figure for Mary. It confirmed the line of David, from Jesse, his father, through the Virgin to Christ the King.

The Fathers no doubt saw little difference between these prophetic anticipations and the miraculous occasions of Old Testament history, which were also to supply a rich source of Marian figures. The best known is perhaps the burning bush of Exodus (3), which Moses observed to be in flames, yet was not consumed, just as the Virgin, who was enlightened by the fire of the Holy Spirit, was not violated by the flames of concupiscence. Other miraculous types for the Virgin Birth were found in Aaron's rod (Numb. 17), which was placed barren in the tabernacle, yet budded, flowered, and formed almonds; and Gideon's fleece (Judg. 6), which the Lord covered with dew and then caused to remain dry as a sign of the power with which he invested Gideon to deliver Israel out of captivity. The latter figure anticipates both the defeat of demons and the triumph of the faithful through the agency of the Virgin, the dew being a received type of Christ.[33]

The majority of the Marian types are, however, purely "symbolic," and many derive from the oldest of all Christian allegories, the Song of Solomon. This erotic epithalamium, applied from early times to the nuptials of Christ and His Church, could equally refer to the Virgin, for she and the Church were mystically one: "Mary stands for the Church, who, when she was betrothed to Christ, as a virgin conceived us of the Holy Spirit, and as a virgin gave birth" (Isidore, LXXXIII.117). The Incarnation and the founding of the terrestrial Church, in which all Christians are conceived, are simultaneous acts, and Mary's role as Mother of Christ, on the occasion of His conception, is, according to St. Ephrem,[34] mystically identical with her title of Bride, on the occasion of His sanctification, as is suggested by the antiphonal phrase: "Ex tuo jam Christus processit alvo, tanquam sponsus de thalamo." [35] Hence all the terms which luxuriantly

33. See Rabanus Maurus (CXI.328) and the famous Middle English song, "I Sing of a Maiden," *Religious Lyrics of the XVth Century,* ed. Carleton Brown (Oxford, 1939), p. 119, No. 81.

34. Thomas S. Livius, *The Blessed Virgin in the Fathers of the First Six Centuries* (London, 1893), p. 383.

35. "From your womb then Christ came forth, as a bridegroom from his chamber." (Translations from the Liturgy and from the Vulgate are mine, with considerable borrowing from authorized translations, where available.)

adorn the "Bride of Christ" in the Canticle become types of Mary: "the flower of the field and the lily of the valleys" (2:1), "the lily among thorns" (2:2), "the tower of David" (4:4), "a garden enclosed, a fountain sealed up" (4:12), "fair as the moon, bright as the sun" (6:9), and so forth.

Other Old Testament images are included in the Marian catalogue and often in new combinations, which, based on concrete figural resemblances, then provide a fresh doctrinal emphasis. In the process the demands of the visual image are often suppressed. A fine illustration is the figure of the "gates of the Temple," which the *Advent* poet alludes to in the eighth division (251) and then elaborates fully in the next (301 ff.). Mary is the "Templum Dei" which Solomon consecrated to contain the Ark of the Covenant and which the glory of the Lord filled with a mighty cloud (II Chron. 5). But she is equally the closed gate of the ideal temple in Ezechiel's vision: "the gate of the outward sanctuary which looked toward the east," of which the Lord said, "This gate shall be shut, it shall not be opened, and no man shall pass through it; because the Lord God of Israel has entered in by it, and it shall be shut" (44:1–2). As God-bearer, Mary is the Temple, and in token of her eternal virginity the gates of her womb are closed by her Son and Lord. St. Ambrose comments on this and numerous other Marian images in the *De institutione virginis* (XVI.319–21). The passage nicely complements Augustine's interpretation of the Exodus figures, where the single typological event was related to Christ and the operation of His sacrament on the sins of the baptized. Here Ambrose gathers images from many sources, maintaining a coherence of doctrinal reference in the elaboration of a complex antitype, the Incarnation, but seriously violating the narrative context of the original images.

Ambrose first confirms the significance of the gates by relating the image to several powerful types of Christ, all of which are, incidentally, part of the figural fabric of the *Advent*. The door looked toward the East, "because He Who poured forth the true light, also engendered the rising Sun [*Oriens*] and gave birth to the Sun of Justice." "A closed gate art thou, O, Virgin," he continues, "Let none open thy gate, which once for all 'Sanctus et Verus' shut, 'Who holds the Key of David; when He opens none may shut; when He shuts none may open.'" By a striking metamorphosis, the closed gate has become the gates of heaven. As the disobedience of Eve had denied us entrance to Paradise, so Mary in her humility reopened the portals to the faithful. The miraculously closed gate of the Virgin, through which the incarnate Word passed, is mystically identified with the golden gates of heaven, through which Christ descended to assume human form. By the faith and consent of Mary and the miracle of the

Virgin Birth, the necessary historical context was provided for the accomplishment of man's salvation and the undoing of Eve's transgression. With such a pattern of interwoven doctrine and typology, it was possible to say that the closed gate opened the golden gates of Paradise.

Typology in the Middle Ages, then, extended far beyond the limits suggested by the New Testament. It came to involve almost any person or place, animal or object, in the Old Testament. It may be said also to incorporate much of the paraphernalia of what is commonly called allegory. Indeed, in many minds, medieval and modern, it is indistinguishable from allegory, or, at the least, a distinction is drawn between "historical" and "symbolic" typology.[36] Such differences, however, were seldom sharply felt after the early patristic period. Most medieval believers found in typology more than just a way of reading the Bible. It was a function of that revelation, established in faith, of God's pervasive purpose, which might be perceived in His inspired Scriptures as well as throughout His Creation. It was a vehicle of meditation in which the accord between terrestrial image and spiritual reality was insured by centuries of theological and liturgical tradition. In writers like Ambrose and Augustine it promoted a kind of imaginative logic according to which one linked image with image in a demonstration of the coherence of the articles of Christian faith. Such an imaginative structure could stand on an equal footing with theological argument, for the integrity of eternal reality was no more clearly apparent in abstract dogma than in the written or visible figures of revealed truth.

No wonder, then, that typological patterns became the staple not only of exegetes and theologians, of liturgists and homilists, but also of the artists of the Church, whether the medium was plastic or verbal. One need only recall that the Gothic cathedral was itself a vast typological program which the architects and then the sculptors worked out in the minutest detail. The statuary of Chartres, for example, is so arranged that it forms a schematic replica of human history from Creation to Judgment, and the stained glass of its windows is commonly organized on typological rather than narrative principles. Illuminators of manuscripts, too, filled their allotted space with symbolic scenes and figures, and were often not content until they had filled the margins with types or "contra-types" of the central illustration. Toward the end of the Middle Ages they produced great compendia like the *Speculum humanae salvationis* and the *Biblia pauperum,* in which the poor man could not only read in pictures the

36. See Woollcombe's discussion in *Essays in Typology,* pp. 69 ff.

major events of scriptural history but could also see them surrounded in resplendent fashion by their typological counterparts.

Among the verbal arts it would not be hard to find examples of typological thinking in such quasi-literary forms as sermons, devotional handbooks, and mystical tracts. But since these, for the most part, merely duplicate the manner and material already illustrated from the Fathers, it will be economical if we turn directly to our primary interest, poetry. In selecting literary examples, I have tried to repeat my earlier sequence of typological kinds (from event to object) and of antitypes (from Christ to Mary) by which I rehearsed the possibilities in scriptural exegesis. That one may do so is of some interest in itself, a testimony to the pervasiveness of typological material in literature. This is not my first concern, however. A literary work may appropriate figures from Scripture, but it is obliged to create a new context and a new structure to contain them. The examples which follow will suggest ways in which typological matter may influence the imaginative form of the poem that incorporates it. Because the *Advent* is in some respects a most intricate work, I have chosen to reserve consideration of its structure for a separate chapter and have begun with shorter texts of fairly simple and obvious formal procedure. Because of the limitations of the Old English poetic canon I have had to range far into the Middle English period. I trust that the anachronism of this excursus will not obscure the relevance of its theoretical determinations to an Old English poem. Typology is not confined, of course, even to the Middle Ages, but throughout that various epoch it had widespread currency, while its imaginative character remained basically unchanged.

LITERARY TYPOLOGY

Typological references are abundant in the shorter religious lyrics as well as in more ambitious poetic structures, but probably the best place to find occurrences of strict historical types is in the mystery plays. This should come as no surprise, given their origin in the liturgy, the milieu in which typological imagery thrives. Furthermore, some of the clerical playwrights must have thought of the Corpus Christi cycle as something like an animated *Biblia pauperum,* combining the scope of all human history with the resonance of redemptive typology.

The fact that a Prophets' Play was a fixture of most of these performances confirms their involvement in the theory of correspondences out of which historical typology grew. The *Ordo Prophetarum* [37] was originally a procession of Messianic prophecies, but in one English cycle [38] the Prophets are joined to a line of kings who together make up a living "Tree of Jesse." "Isaias" opens the pageant with the "Emmanuel" prophecy. "Radix Jesse" is the second speaker:

> A blyssyd braunch xal sprynge of me
> That xal be swettere þan bawmys breth
> Out of þat braunch in nazareth
> A flowre xal blome of me jesse rote
> The whych by grace xal dystroye deth
> And brynge mankende to blysse most sote.   (17–22)

The proclamation of "Jonas propheta" is a perfect example of simple Christian prefiguration, the point of correspondence being, of course, the Resurrection:

> I jonas sey þat on þe iij[de] morn
> ffro deth he xal ryse þis is a trew tall
> fyguryd in me þe which longe beforn
> lay iij days beryed with in þe quall.   (67–70)

The Old Testament subjects in the large cycles were chosen not for their dramatic potentiality but for crucial historical importance. As turning points in the chronicle of God's chosen people, they are inevitably of great typological significance. This is particularly evident in a few of the early Towneley Plays, where the primitive dramaturgy reflects a strikingly different rationale from the naturalistic involvement of the plays of the "Wakefield Master." The plays of Isaac (V) and Jacob (VI), for example, read like crude dramatizations of the *Cursor mundi*. The entire emphasis is upon a showing forth of the historical event, with no interest in character or dramatic values. The scene of "Jacob's Pillow" becomes clearly a type of the establishment of the Church. Though Jacob is merely paraphrasing Scripture, the typological implications are unmistakable in the dramatist's isolation of the incident, almost like a tableau:

37. For the origin of this play, see Karl Young, *The Drama of the Medieval Church* (Oxford, 1933), chap. 21. Auerbach (*Typologische Motive*, pp. 18 ff.) points out the lack of distinction between prophets (in the limited sense) and typological figures.

38. *Ludus Coventriae, or the Plaie called Corpus Christi,* ed. K. S. Block (London, 1922), pp. 57–62.

And I Iacob, thi trew hyne,
This stone I rayse in sygne to day
shall I hold holy kyrk for ay;
And of all that newes me
rightwys tend shall I gif the.   (54–58) [39]

In most of the Chester Plays there is a similar indifference to theatricality, but the heavy pedagogical hand of the pious author is even more evident. In the Barbers' Play of Abraham and Melchisedech [40] the actors are accompanied by an "Expositor" on horseback, who expounds "apertlie, / that lewed, standing hereby, / may knowe what this may be" (114–16). He showers indeed a bewildering amount of typological learning upon the heads of the groundlings: Abraham is the Father of heaven, and his offering is the New Testament; Melchisedech is his priest, ministering the sacrament:

In the old lawe, without leasing,
when these two good men were lyving,
of beastes was all their offring
and eck their sacramente.
but sith Christ dyed on the roode tree,
with bread and wyne him worship we,
and on Sherthursday in his maundye
was his Comaundment.

But for this thinge vsed shold be
afterward as now done wee,
in signification, as leve you me,
Melchisedech did soe;
and tythes-makinge, as you se here,
of Abraham begunnen were.
therfore he was to God full deare,
and so were they both twoo.   (121–36)

The inconsistency of God the Father paying tithes and receiving the sacrament seems to have left the Expositor unconcerned, and he rides on through the remaining vignettes of Abraham's career, pedantically announcing the circumcision to be a type of Baptism, and the sacrificial offering of Isaac a prefiguration of the Crucifixion.

39. *The Towneley Plays,* ed. George England (London, 1897), p. 53.
40. *The Chester Plays,* ed. Hermann Deimling (London, 1892), pp. 63–69.

It has long been observed that Langland's handling of the magnificent scenes in the final passus of *Piers Plowman* (B XVIII-XX) betrays some familiarity with the medieval theatre. Perhaps, in one instance at least, that influence extends to the association of typological patterns with the climactic moments in Christian history. In the terrifying debate with the Powers of hell over the souls of the Patriarchs and Prophets in limbo, the "Anima Christi" invokes the Irenaean doctrine of recapitulation in defense of His behavior. Citing the dictum of the Old Law, He piles correspondence upon correspondence in thundering justification of the divine Atonement:

> *Dentem pro dente, et oculum pro oculo.*
> *Ergo,* soule shal soule quyte · and synne to synne wende,
> And al that man hath mysdo · I, man, wyl amende.
> Membre for membre · bi the olde lawe was amendes,
> And lyf for lyf also · and by that lawe I clayme it,
> Adam and al his issue · at my wille her-after.
> And that deth in hem fordid · my deth shal releue,
> And bothe quykke and quyte · that queynte was thorw synne . . .
>
> And I, in lyknesse of a leode · that lorde am of heuene,
> Graciousliche thi gyle haue quytte · go gyle aʒeine gyle!
> And as Adam and alle · thorw a tre deyden,
> Adam and alle thorwe a tree · shal torne aʒeine to lyue;
> And gyle is bigyled · and in his gyle fallen.[41]

Just as the historical types for Christ, the Church, and the sacraments seem to be readily available in the dramatic literature, so for illustration of the symbolic or allegorical types the lyrics addressed to the Virgin come first to mind. Chaucer, probably as a youthful exercise, translated from the French of de Guilleville an alphabetical prayer [42] which contains the figures of the burning bush, "signe of thin unwemmed maidenhede" (91), the "temple devout, ther God hath his woninge" (145), and the open well (Zech. 13:1) "to wasshe sinful soule out of his gilt" (178). In the Prologue to the *Prioress' Tale,*[43] however, the Marian figures are given some structural importance. The second stanza addresses the Virgin as the

41. *Piers the Plowman,* ed. W. W. Skeat (London, 1924), B-Text, xviii, 338–43, 354–58, p. 544. The title, "Anima Christi," is alluded to in line 304 and may be a further echo of the mystery cycles. See, for example, *The Chester Plays,* pp. 305 ff.

42. *Works,* pp. 524–26.

43. Ibid., p. 161.

"white lylye flour" (461), and the third as the "bussh unbrent, brennynge in Moyses sighte" (468), shifting the emphasis from simple virginity to virgin maternity. With the additional titles conferred by the next two stanzas, the invocation is given a kind of ascending progression—Virgin, Mother, Lady, Queen—which suggests a recapitulation of the career of Mary from the Annunciation to the Coronation and provides a suitable crescendo of praise and honor.

By far the commonest lyric structure in the late Middle Ages for an address to the Virgin was this sort of catalogue of images.[44] Generally, however, there was no attempt at further organization; the effect sought was apparently that of a typological litany. The anonymous fourteenth-century lyric beginning "Marye, mayde mylde and fre" [45] represents such a pattern at its purest. Of the fourteen stanzas only the first and last contain the petition, while the others (more than seventy lines) merely fill out a register of well-known types in a somewhat perfunctory fashion: "chambre of þe trynyte" (2), "Queen of paradise" (7), "coluere of Noe" (dove, 13), "bosche of Synay" (19), "þe rytte Sarray" (the legitimate Sarah, 20), the "sling of David" (25), the "rod of Aaron" (27), the "temple of Solomon" (31), "Judith" (37), "Esther" (43), the "closed gate" (51), "Rachel" (53), the "hill of Daniel" (55), the "unicorn" (63), and the "woman clothed with the Sun" (Apoc. 12:1, 68). The sheer weight of the ornamental incrustation must have had an appeal like that of the jeweled and gilded crucifix or reliquary, but the structural significance of the typology is negligible.

Though the versification is considerably more sophisticated, the same aesthetic principle lies behind many of the religious lyrics of John Lydgate. The aureate diction blends unobtrusively with the Latin tags and the exotic imagery, to create a lush texture which effectively embellishes and distracts from the simplicity of the structure:

> Haile, holsom cypres, growyng in Syon!
>   Haile, fons signatus, most clere in cristallyne!
> Haile, gold in Trone of prudent Salamon
>   Gostly closed, most hevenly in devyne!

---

44. Catalogues of the joys, sorrows, virtues, etc., of the Virgin were also exceedingly popular.

45. *Religious Lyrics of the XIVth Century,* ed. Carleton Brown, 2d rev. ed. G. V. Smithers (Oxford, 1947), pp. 46–49, No. 32. Auerbach (*Typologische Motive,* pp. 17–18) mentions familiar analogues in the Latin hymnology from the late Carolingian Notker Balbulus to Adam of St. Victor in the 12th century.

    Haile, to-fore whose brest alle grace dide shyne,
From phebus paleys, bilded supra sidera;
    Haile, hevenly gardyn, welle in divyne,
Haile, flos campi, o Ave Iesse virgula! [46]

Lydgate seems to have been fond of these typological exercises and ex-
pended great ingenuity upon them. In his translation of the Latin hymn
"Gloriosa dicta sunt de te" [47] he elaborates the prophetic images of Jerusalem as a prefiguration of the Celestial City, while simultaneously developing both as types of the Virgin, even to the point of relating allegori-
cally the twelve precious stones of the city's foundation to the faith and
virtues of her in whom the Lord chose to rest.

A less concentrated but equally imaginative expansion of Marian figures
is permitted by the leisurely unfolding of Lydgate's *Life of Our Lady*. An
invocation of 63 lines is devoted to the "star" image, which begins as part
of a literal winter landscape and, passing through several metaphorical
transformations, concludes as the illuminating force, as well as the subject, of the poet's composition. The first chapter, "The Nativity of Our
Lady," begins by playing most gracefully upon the "flos campi" figure:

    A Flour of vertue full longe kepyt in cloose
    Full many ver with holsome leves swote
    Only by grace vppon the stalke aroos
    Out of Iesse, spryngnyg fro the Rote
    Off god ordeynyde to be a Resort and bote
    Vnto mankynde our trouble to determyne
    Full longe afforne by prescyens dyvyne

    The wiche Floure, preservithe man from dethe
    Vnto the vertue, who so luste take hede
    That in a garden, a myddys of Nazareth

46. *The Minor Poems of John Lydgate,* I, ed. Henry Noble MacCracken
(London, 1911), p. 299.

47. Ibid., pp. 315–23. Some of the other Marian lyrics relying heavily upon
typological patterns are the "Ballade at the Reverence of Our Lady, Qwene of
Mercy," "To Mary, the Queen of Heaven," "Ave Regina Celorum," and "Ave,
Jesse Virgula," of which the second stanza is cited above. Other subjects are, of
course, abundant. See, for example, "A Seying of the Nightingale," pp. 232–33,
in which Lydgate enumerates ten types of the Cross of Christ, concluding with
David's sling, of which the five stones are the five wounds by which Christ
vanquished Satan.

So fayre som tyme gan to spryng and sprede
That thorough the worlde bothe in lenthe and brede
The fresshe odour, and also the swetnesse
Hertes comforteth, of all her hevynesse   (64–77) [48]

There follows an apostrophe to Nazareth, which the royalty of this "Flower" has raised above the famed cities of the classical world; next, a recollection of the prophecy of Isaiah that the Holy Ghost should rest upon this "Flower"; following this, a composite picture of this white lily, unfading rose, and violet of mercy and pity; then, an allusion to the miracle at the Golden Gate, where the "stock," Joachim and Anna, learned of their "Flower's" origin; and finally, only with the birth of Mary does the narrative drop the image of the "frute so holy and entere," but then begins another extended typological rhapsody, this time on the theme of the orient light of dawn, which dispersed the night of deadly error. This long sweep of figural development allows the poet a display of classical and scriptural learning as well as some precise allegorical explication, all elegantly unified in a single image which is both authoritative and richly appropriate to the occasion, the birth of the Mother of God.

Lydgate's method in the *Life of the Virgin* depends upon variation of the typological figure—scriptural allusion to flowers, the structural parts and the qualities of the flower—but the referent, or antitype, remains the same. The inverse of this procedure can be fruitfully illustrated by the Old English poem *The Phoenix*,[49] in which the author has chosen a Latin text to provide him with a single, though elaborate, figural basis.

First, a word of explanation may be in order. The example may seem far afield in a discussion of typology, for the *Carmen de ave phoenice,* attributed to Lactantius, is a late classical and predominantly pagan poem. It might be assumed that the authority of divine inspiration is the minimal requirement for even "symbolic" typology, and that *The Phoenix* would more accurately be termed an allegory. Yet there are two elements in the Old English poem which show how little such categorical distinctions meant to the medieval poet. The first justification is in the scriptural author-

---

48. *A Critical Edition of John Lydgate's "Life of Our Lady"*, ed. Joseph A. Lauritis, Ralph A. Klinefelter, and Vernon F. Gallagher (Pittsburgh, 1961), pp. 251–52.

49. The edition cited is N. F. Blake, ed., *The Phoenix* (Manchester, 1964). I have, however, restored two traditional emendations in lines 648–50, where Blake retains what he considers a late Old English textual tradition.

ity he does provide, and the second is the method by which he unifies the
two parts of his poem.

The Old English text paraphrases the Latin poem rather systematically
in its first 380 lines; then, in the second part, it offers a Christian interpretation for the wondrous legend of the phoenix. The transition between
the two parts seems to have been inspired by the final line of Lactantius'
work, "Aeternam vitam mortis adepta bono," which no Christian reader
could have failed to apply to his own beliefs. The Old English version
makes explicit the meaning of the mysterious gift of the phoenix, by which
it might rise again from ashes to a renewed life of youthful vigor:

> Swa þæt ece lif   eadigra gehwylc
> æfter sarwræce   sylf geceoseð
> þurh deorcne deað,   þæt he Dryhtnes mot
> æfter geardagum   geofona neotan
> on sindreamum   ond siþþan a
> wunian in worulde   weorca to leane.   (381–86)

[Thus each of the blessed ones, after great misery, chooses for himself
eternal life through dark death, that he may, after his former days, enjoy
the gifts of God in perpetual bliss and thereafter dwell forever in that
world as a reward for his works.]

But in the midst of his explication the poet challenges those who might
think that he is trading in feigned fables, *þæt ic lygewordum leoð somnige,
write woðcræfte* (547–48a). In support of his exegesis of a secular legend,
he cites the inspired words of Job:

> "Ic þæt ne forhycge   heortan geþoncum
> þæt ic in minum neste   neobed ceose,
> hæle hrawerig,   gewite hean þonan
> on longne sið   lame bitolden
> geomor gudæda   in greotes fæðm,
> ond þonne æfter deaþe   þurh Dryhtnes giefe
> swa se fugel fenix   feorh edniwe
> æfter æriste   agan mote,
> dreamas mid Dryhten,   þær seo deore scolu
> Leofne lofiað."   (552–61a)

[I do not scorn in my heart's thoughts to choose a deathbed in my nest,
a man weary in body, to go wretched then on a long journey, covered

with dust, lamenting past deeds, into the embrace of earth, and then after death, through the gift of God, like the bird phoenix, I may possess a renewed body after resurrection, bliss with the Lord, where the cherished throng praise the Beloved.]

Though it is surprising to discover this reading of Job 29:18 in an Anglo-Saxon poem,[50] it is clear that the poet is both reinforcing his spiritual exegesis by the example of Job and justifying his use of a nonscriptural authority. Job, like the phoenix, is the type of the good Christian who, despite his suffering, kept faith with God and can hope for eternal life. As Blake points out, "it is fitting therefore that Job's song should echo the phoenix's." [51] In addition, the fact that an inspired Prophet referred to the phoenix as a figure for his condition provides the poet's handling of a secular poem on the subject with an authoritative typological precedent.

Furthermore, in the treatment of the phoenix material the poet departs regularly from his source to place the legend in the context of Christian history. Blake, in his fine edition of the poem, has stressed the numerous ways in which the poet, in telling the story, prepares for the interpretation which is to follow.[52] The ornate mythological allusions of the Latin are replaced by simple but insistent references to sacred history. The paradise in which the phoenix dwells is reserved for the blessed (11–12), and the sinful are excluded (5b–6). In the second part the connection with Eden is explained: the sin and expulsion of Adam and Eve have placed Paradise remote from men, *afyrred . . . þurh Meotudes meaht,* but it may become again the haunt of the chosen, as it is for the phoenix, if their faith

50. The Vulgate reads: "In nidulo meo moriar, et sicut palma multiplicabo dies." Sister Mary Francis McDonald, in her translation of *Lactantius: The Minor Works* (Washington, D.C., 1965), p. 208, points out that the translation of the new Confraternity edition, "based, no doubt, heavily on Hebraic tradition, is appreciably the appropriate one here": "In my own nest I shall grow old; I shall multiply years like the phoenix." The Septuagint or any Greek text would have been ambiguous, since the Greek word "phoinix" means "palm tree" as well as the bird "phoenix." Sister McDonald has found no significant reading in Old Latin texts to place against the accepted "palma" of the Vulgate. The Old English poet's information might, however, have come from a commentary, such as that of Gregory the Great in his *Moralia* 19 (see McDonald, p. 208, n. 8) or that on Job attributed by Bede to Philip the Presbyter (see Blake, p. 21).

51. *The Phoenix,* p. 84.

52. See Blake's "Introduction: The Form," ibid., pp. 24–35, and the Notes, passim.

is great enough. The paradise is a part of the divine plan: all things are beautiful and beneficent *swa him God bibead* (36b). The place, like its legendary and symbolic inhabitants, is seen in relation to apocalyptic history. Having survived the Flood (41b–46), it will succumb to the fires of the Last Judgment (40b–41a, 46–49, 242a). All is in the power of the Lord its Creator:

> Þæt onwended ne bið
> æfre to ealdre,   ærþon endige
> frod fyrngeweorc   se hit on frymþe gescop.   (82b–84)

[That shall never be changed at any time, until He Who created it in the beginning shall put an end to the ancient, long-established work.]

The activities of the phoenix are described as the appropriate response to such a habitation. The bird is a worshiper of the sun, the symbol of Creation, *torht tacen Godes* (96a). It is also the sun that brings about the immolation which renews the life of this creature, whose generative processes are one of the mysteries of the Creator:

> God ana wat,
> Cyning ælmihtig   hu his gecynde bið,
> wifhades þe weres;   þæt ne wat ænig
> monna cynnes   butan Meotod ana
> hu þa wisan sind   wundorlice,
> fæger fyrngesceap   ymb þæs fugles gebyrd.   (355b–60)

[Only God, the almighty King, knows what its sex is, female or male; none of mankind knows except God alone, what were the wondrous dispositions, the fair, ancient decrees, concerning the bird's nature.]

In the poet's eyes, then, not only is his fable vested with scriptural authority, but it is manifestly a type of the essential mysteries of human history from Creation to Resurrection to Judgment. To a poet who was willing to credit the phoenix legend as a true and significant revelation of the divine plan, the differentiation of his exegesis from historical typology would have been a pointless distinction.

The immediate relevance of *The Phoenix* to this argument, however, lies in the poet's typological method, which involves a daring reduplication of the antitype. He is not content with one interpretation of the phoenix legend, although it involves a thorough recapitulation of the complex details. The primary significance concerns the lives of those good Christians who "make their nest" in Christ. Bringing the pleasant plants of their good deeds, they rise in flame, purged of the sins of earthly life, their souls bearing the renewed body to eternal glory with the Redeemer. But the phoenix is also a figure for Christ Himself, around Whom the lesser birds flock (591–94a), as they did when the phoenix manifested himself to the world in his resurrected state. This interpretation becomes explicit in the final portion of the poem where the subject is the Resurrection:

> Swa fenix beacnað
> geong in geardum Godbearnes meaht
> þonne he of ascan eft onwæcneð
> in lifes lif leomum geþungen.
> Swa se Hælend us *h*elpe gefremede,
> þurh his lices gedal lif butan ende,
> swa se fugel swetum his fiþru tu
> ond wynsumum wyrtum gefylleð,
> fægrum foldwæstmum þonne afysed bið. (646b–54)

[Thus the phoenix signifies, young in his dwelling, the might of the Son of God, when he awakes again from the ashes to the life of life, vigorous in his limbs. As the Savior brought us help, through the death of His body life without end, so the bird fills his two wings with sweet and pleasant spices, with the fair fruits of the earth, when he is impelled.]

The multiple reference of the phoenix ought not to seem confusing or be written off as a failure on the poet's part to organize his material, as Blake suggests.[53] It is, on the contrary, another instance of the fertile energy of typological imagining. Just as a figure may be formally multiplied while the referent remains stable, so the simple type may be unchanged while its significance undergoes repeated alteration. The process ought never to be pointless, however, for as in one case unity of form—"gates" or "flowers"—is maintained, in the other, conceptual unity provides a coherent, enriched pattern. The phoenix may represent both God and man simultaneously, because in the Creation of man and the Incarnation of the Lord, such a similitude was historically realized. By the Resurrection of Christ in human form, body and spirit, the pattern for the resurrection of man was made a part of the history of human experience. Therefore it is not only possible but inevitable that a symbol for one will be equally valid for the other. By the logic of typology, in which type and antitype are

53. See ibid., pp. 33–35.

formally identical parts of the historical process, a figure which serves for
the redeemed will necessarily serve for the Redeemer, since either antitype is part of the same pattern of historical realization. The shift in the
meaning of the phoenix figure is merely apparent and, within the structure
of typological imagining, ought to create no greater confusion than the
shift from one flower to another. More often than not, it is the inflexibility
of the modern critic which is at fault, rather than the capacities of the
medieval poet. Educated in the mobile conventions of scriptural exegesis,
the medieval imagination found in the configurations of belief the design
for a flexible, many-faceted art.

These, then, are some of the ways in which typological patterns can
supply the foundation for poetic structures. We have moved from mere allusion, implicit or defined, along the familiar range of Christian types to
the catalogues of Marian figures, with some suggestion of the structural
sophistication they permit. Finally, in *The Phoenix,* we have seen the
corollary of this extravagant display of imagery—a figural economy combined with doctrinal multiplicity. These illustrations, however, do little
justice to that complexity of typological meditation which one finds in the
writings of the great Doctors of the early Church. The Old English *Advent,*
to which we may now devote our full attention, will prove a splendid example of a sizable poetic structure whose coherence depends upon the
traditions of patristic typology. Though basically typological figures function much like the imagery of any verbal structure, the difference lies in
the way in which tenor and vehicle are related to one another and to
others in the same poem, in order to form a cohesive structure. The difference here may be attributed to the awareness of an authority which
transcends the poet's imaginative act, to the historical perspective by which
that authority is understood, and to the traditional explication of those
Scriptures in which sacred history is recorded. The *Advent* may seem
a rather short poem—when measured against, say, the *Divine Comedy*—
to merit the weighty commentary which follows. It is, however, a work
of some figural density and in a mode that we can appreciate only im-
perfectly. A survey of the attempts to define the formal structure of the
Advent will make clear how foreign to contemporary criticism have been
the imaginative principles which this chapter has sought to define and
illustrate in both primary and secondary manifestations. The relatively uncomplicated devices of poetic organization which have concerned us thus
far are merely extended and multiplied in the *Advent,* but there are
special problems raised by a non-discursive, non-narrative poem of some

length and complexity, to which we must now address ourselves. I trust that the exegetical and literary examples of this chapter will, however, permit us to retain a sense of the essential simplicity of the typological imagination.

2. THE ADVENT SEQUENCE

In te, anime meus, tempora mea metior. Affec-
tionem, quam res praetereuntes in te faciunt, et
cum illae praeterierint, manet, ipsam metior
praesentem, non ea quae praeterierunt, ut fieret.

St. Augustine

THE STRUCTURE OF THE *ADVENT* AS A POETIC UNIT HAS BEEN twice obscured by editorial procedure, first by inclusion in the *Christ* triptych, then by fragmentation into a group of lyrics. Cook, in his edition of 1900, was much exercised to demonstrate Cynewulfian authorship and hence the unity of the first three poems of the *Exeter Book*. He seems to have been little concerned about the coherence of the initial poem, beyond that accorded by the Advent theme and the antiphonal sources. In speaking of the latter, however, he acknowledges what might be taken as a kind of formal satisfaction. The poet, he says,

abridged, expanded, suppressed, or transposed, as his genius dictated; freely interpolated matter from other sources, when it suited his purpose so to do; and welded the whole together by closing with a magnificent doxology to the triune God, followed by a few resumptive lines in which, returning to the theme of Advent, he alludes to the reward which Christ will bestow upon the righteous at his second appearing. (pp. xlii-iii)

But Cook's conclusion—that since the poem is "essentially lyrical in character . . . the only unity demanded is that secured through the character of the Advent season to which the Antiphons belong" (p. xci)—proved somewhat awkward when examined in detail by Smithson in his study, *The Old English Christian Epic*.[1] Postulating a principle of lyric unity, a unity of mood dependent upon the emotional appeal of the lyric, he was obliged to concede a violation of that principle by those passages of the poem which are "manifestly expository" and "appeal primarily to the intellect" (p. 325). This defective unity is, he continues, further disturbed by "abrupt changes of style or method of presentation" (pp. 326–27); the pleasant variety which the poet has achieved is attained only at the expense of a "congruity of tone." Above all, he laments the "lack of definite

1. G. A. Smithson, *The Old English Christian Epic,* University of California Publications in Modern Philology, I, No. 4 (Berkeley, 1910).

order or arrangement of material." Though the individual sections of the *Advent* display an excellent organization, the poem as a whole is merely a "series of lyric outbursts thrown together at random" (p. 335), demonstrating "an absolute lack of the sense for larger coherence, of the restraint in the midst of lyric fervor which determines the structural plan of the whole" (p. 336).

The title of Jackson J. Campbell's edition of 1959, *The Advent Lyrics of the Exeter Book,* immediately advertizes an equal unhappiness with attempts to discern formal coherence, outside of the individual poems, in what he considers a collection of "indoctrination pieces." He finds himself "forced to the conclusion that there is no structural progression in idea or emotion from one poem to the next." Rather like Cook, he is willing to let the organization rest upon the linking of Advent themes, to which he adds the repetition of lyric pattern:

> There are . . . certain recurring ideas which appear from time to time like *leit motifs*: the coexistence of the Father and the Son, the purity of Mary, the miracle of the virgin birth, Man's inability to understand God's mysteries, his misery and need for Grace, and the necessity for rendering abundant praise and glory to God. These themes appear irregularly, and weave themselves into no observable pattern of thematic structure, yet they do provide connecting links of a sort from poem to poem, and they, along with the obvious similarities of formal lyric structure, serve to unify the whole group. (p. 10)

Thus neither the "lyric mood" nor the thematic material of the Advent season is in itself accounted a sufficiently sturdy structural principle. Yet few readers will, I think, agree with Campbell's statement that, with the exception of the final piece, "the order of the poems is unimportant" (p. 11). In spite of the abrupt shifts of tone and matter between the sections, one senses a control of the formal problems which extends beyond the individual pieces. As in some of the sonnet sequences and meditative collections of later centuries, there is a grander scheme of thought and feeling which overrides the constrictions of the shorter form. Something of this larger pattern may be better apprehended if the poems are understood in terms of the typological associations they inherited from their sources.

As in the case of *The Phoenix* and indeed much of Old English religious poetry, the sources of the *Advent* sequence are in part clearly ascertainable and in part uncertain. Where the poet was using recognized liturgical material, he paraphrased and expanded with considerable freedom. Where no specific source has been discovered, we must, in our ignorance of early liturgical matters, allow for the possibility of lost or unrecovered manuscripts. On the other hand, we cannot, in an excess of historical conservatism, deny a poet of acknowledged mastery the privilege of independent creation. Yet, since all but two of the divisions have some identifiable inspiration in antiphons of the final week of Advent or soon thereafter,[2] it seems best to assume that the poet was either using primary antiphonal material throughout, or at least deliberately casting his work in an antiphonal mold. The particular source problems attending each section will be discussed in the commentary which follows, but the general character of these antiphons requires preliminary exploration.

The "Antiphonae Majores" or "Great O's" constitute a high point of the impressive Advent liturgy and are celebrated with great solemnity. According to Guéranger,[3] they were sung at Vespers, because it was at the evening of the world, "vergente mundi vespere," that the Messiah came, and attached to the Magnificat, to indicate that the awaited Savior will come to us through Mary. The antiphons were repeated before and after the Canticle as on double feasts, a sign of the highest solemnity; in the ancient usage of some Churches they were chanted before the Magnificat, before the Gloria Patri, and after the "Sicut erat." In the *Liber responsalis sive Antiphonarius* of Gregory the Great (LXXVIII.732–33) they are found in the following order for the week preceding the Feast of the Nativity:

> O Sapientia, quae ex ore Altissimi prodiisti, attingens a fine usque ad finem, fortiter suaviter disponensque omnia: veni ad docendum nos viam prudentiae.

2. The source of lines 416–21, the antiphon *O admirabile commercium,* is included in the Gregorian *Liber responsalis sive Antiphonarius* (LXXVIII. 741) for Vespers of the Vigil of the Octave of our Lord, the close of the Nativity celebration. The antiphons associated with lines 378–415 have been frequently assigned to the Sundays following the feast of the Epiphany. See Dom Edward Burgert, *The Dependence of Part I of Cynewulf's Christ upon the Antiphonary* (Washington, D.C., 1921), p. 44.

3. Dom Prosper Guéranger, *L'Année liturgique: L'Avent* (13th ed. Paris, 1896), p. 535. Rosemary Woolf admonishes against the anachronistic use of this work in her review of Campbell's edition, *MÆ, 29* (1960), 125–29: It was "not intended to be a precise, objective study of mediaeval liturgies with their diversities of practice, but was rather designed to arouse a devotional understanding of the Roman liturgy" (p. 126). My citations are meant merely to recall something of the solemnity associated with these antiphons during the course of the Middle Ages, and not to suggest a specific Anglo-Saxon usage known to our poet.

O Adonai, dux domus Israel, qui Moysi in igne flammae rubi apparuisti, et ei in Sina legem dedisti: veni ad redimendum nos in brachio extento.

O Radix Jesse, qui stas in signum populorum, super quem reges continebunt os suum, quem gentes deprecabuntur: veni ad liberandum nos, jam noli tardare.

O Clavis David, et sceptrum domus Israel; qui aperis, et nemo claudit, claudis, et nemo aperit: veni, et educ vinctum de domo carceris, sedentem in tenebris, et umbra mortis.

O Oriens, splendor lucis aeternae, et Sol justitiae: veni, et illumina sedentes in tenebris et umbra mortis.

O Rex gentium, et desideratus earum, lapisque angularis, qui facis utraque unum: veni, et salva hominem, quem de limo formasti.

O Emmanuel, Rex et legifer noster, exspectatio gentium, et Salvator earum: veni ad salvandum nos, Dominus Deus noster.[4]

The vocative exclamation with which these antiphons begin is by no means common, being limited largely to these seven and a few others for the same season, probably created on their model. The "O" was explained by the ninth century liturgiologist Amalarius (CV. 1265): " 'O' is the in-

4. "O Wisdom, that proceeds from the mouth of the Most High, reaching from end to end, mightily and sweetly disposing all things, come to teach us the way of prudence.

"O Adonai, and leader of the house of Israel, who appeared to Moses in the fire of the burning bush, and gave him the law on Sinai, come to redeem us by outstretched arm.

"O root of Jesse, who stands as the ensign of the peoples, before whom kings shall not open their mouths, to whom the nations shall pray, come to deliver us, tarry now no more.

"O key of David, and scepter of the house of Israel, who opens and no man shuts, who shuts and no man opens: come and lead the captive from prison, sitting in darkness, and in the shadow of death.

"O Orient, splendor of eternal light, and sun of justice, come and enlighten those who sit in darkness, and in the shadow of death.

"O King of nations, and their desired one, and the cornerstone, that makes both one, come and save man, whom You formed out of dust.

"O Emmanuel, our King and lawgiver, the expectation and Savior of the nations, come to save us, O Lord, our God."

terjection of one in a state of wonderment. By means of that 'O' the singer wished to intimate that the words which follow pertain to some marvelous vision which is better suited to the rumination of the mind than to the discourse of a public speaker."

Following the exclamation of wonder are complex figures for Christ, gleaned from Old Testament prophecy and concentrated with awesome typological potency. The "veni" petitions, which conclude the antiphons, draw out some of the doctrinal implications of this rich imagery. Only the last four of these texts are involved in the surviving fragment of the *Advent,* but these suffice to illustrate the typological imagination at work in their constructing. In the *O Emmanuel* the familiar prophetic name, harbinger of the Incarnation, is further associated with royal titles and activities, while the prayer for salvation unites the expectant present with the past in their dependence upon the "God-with-us." In the other antiphons a more or less enigmatic figure is brought into conjunction with a commonplace one, sparking a new metaphoric vitality and explication or, at the least, directing the significance of the mysterious symbol. The "Day-star" and the "Sun" of *O Oriens* are set against the familiar "shadow of death," and the "Key of David" is related to the "prison house." Similarly, but more obliquely, in the *Rex gentium* antiphon the architectural image of the unifying "Cornerstone" is projected against the formation of man out of mire, thus figuratively associating Redemption with Creation and, by means of the "King of Nations" title, with the founding of the Church. The construction of these "Great O's," then, shows clearly the kind of imaginative process inherited by the *Advent* poet when he contemplated his sources.

During the early Christian centuries the seven "Major Antiphons" of Advent engendered a few others, imitative in structure and content. These "added O's," believed to have been of monastic origin, are found in many medieval antiphonaries, following the "Great Seven" and increasing their number to eight, nine, and frequently twelve.[5] The most venerable of these additions were:

5. See Everard Green, "On the Words O SAPIENTIA in the Kalendar," *Archaeologia, 49* (1885), 220–21. Since the "Great Antiphons" were most frequently performed with the Magnificat at Vespers during the week preceding Christmas and were sufficient in number to those seven days of services, the "monastic O's" must have been relegated to another moment in the liturgy. The exact position must have depended upon local custom. They were, according to Burgert (*Dependence,* p. 70), "more liable to shifting and to individual re-arrangement than even the seven Universal O's." The earliest volume, which contains all of the antiphons relevant to the *Advent,* the 10th-century

O Virgo virginum, quomodo fiet istud? quia nec primam similem visa es, nec habere sequentem. —Filiae Hierusalem, quid me admiramini? Divinum est mysterium hoc quod cernitis.

O Gabriel, nuntius coelorum, qui januis clausis ad me intrasti, et Verbum nuntiasti: Concipies et paries: Emmanuel vocabitur.

O Rex pacifice, tu ante saecula nate: Per auream egredere portam, redemptos tuos visita, et eos illuc revoca unde ruerunt per culpam.

O Hierusalem, civitas Dei summi: Leva in circuitu oculos tuos, et vide Dominum tuum, quia jam veniet solvere te a vinculis.

O mundi Domina, regio ex semine orta: Ex tuo jam Christus processit alvo, tanquam sponsus de thalamo; hic jacet in praesepio qui et sidera regit.[6]

Of these all but the *O Gabriel* are important to the Old English poem in its present form. Four of the "added O's," with four of the "Great O's,"

Antiphonary of Hartker, relegates these additional O's to the service "ad crucem." This rubric is explained by Burgert (pp. 68–70) as a reference to the "commemoration made in Lauds after the 'Benedictus' and in Vespers after the 'Magnificat.' In the English use these antiphons with accompanying prayers are called 'memorials,' and they were always chanted after the regular antiphon and prayer for the day or feast." If these "commemorations" were omitted during the Advent season, they were replaced by special memorials in honor of the Virgin Mary. The antiphons considered here would all have been directly or symbolically appropriate to such a service.

6. "O Virgin of virgins, how shall this be? for never was there one like you, nor will there ever be.—Daughters of Jerusalem, why do you look wondering at me? What you behold is a divine mystery.

"O Gabriel, messenger of the heavens, who entered by the closed gates to me, and announced the Word: You shall conceive and bear a child; he shall be called Emmanuel.

"O King of peace, You who were born before all ages: come out by the golden gate, visit them You have redeemed, and lead them back to that place from which they fell by sin.

"O Jerusalem, city of the great God: lift up your eyes round about, and see your Lord, for soon He will come to release you from your chains.

"O Lady of the world, sprung of royal seed: from your womb Christ came forth, as a bridegroom from his chamber; He lies in a manger who also rules the stars."

provided the sources, or points of departure, for eight of the first nine of the surviving sections of the *Advent*.

This additional material differs noticeably in subject matter: allusion to the Virgin Birth is prominent, and only one antiphon is addressed to Christ directly. The petition is also lacking—a distinction, however, which the Old English poet somewhat obscures in his expansion and adaptation. Still, the striking typological figures are there in full measure: the closed Doors, the golden Gates, the Bridegroom proceeding from the nuptial chamber, and the personified Jerusalem. But the impact of these antiphons is more vivid and immediate, less hieratic and removed from the realized event. The imperatives relate not so much to the plight of the humble petitioner as to a dramatic evocation of the symbol (*O Hierusalem*) or of a specific moment in the life of Mary (the Annunciation in the *O Gabriel* and the Nativity in the *O mundi Domina*) or of an imaginary scene (in the *O Virgo virginem*, the dialogue between Mary and the Daughters of Jerusalem). This extension of the possibilities of the antiphonal structure not only prepares the way for the extraordinary "Passus" section but also liberates the poet's treatment of material from the "Great O's," inviting him to confer dramatic immediacy upon their figures along side of the more austere theological explications.

The order of the "Great Antiphons" found in the so-called Gregorian Antiphonary is that which was accepted in the modern Breviary. It is also the order which predominates in medieval texts, but it is not the only one recorded and certainly not that of the Old English poem. There is no strong evidence that this order has any inherent rationale. The great medieval authorities on the liturgy were fond of associating the seven Antiphons with the seven Gifts of the Holy Spirit. But while Honorius of Autun (CLXXII.644) is able to relate the Gregorian order to the list of Gifts in Isaiah (11:23), Amalarius (CV.1267 ff.), whose study of the antiphons is far more penetrating, finds it necessary to follow an order which was not that of his community. Dom Edward Burgert, in his useful monograph *The Dependence of Part I of Cynewulf's Christ upon the Antiphonary*, discovered two cases of continental Benedictine usage with the minor variation of placing the *Oriens* antiphon at the end of the series. In the order exhibited by the Old English *Advent*, the adjustment is equally minor: the *Rex gentium* is moved up to precede the *Clavis David*. It is more than possible, then, that the Old English poet did not simply present his antiphons, as Dubois [7] suggests, "dans un ordre fan-

7. Marguerite Dubois, *Les Éléments latins dans la poésie religieuse de Cynewulf* (Paris, 1942), p. 85.

taisiste, et sans doute de mémoire," but that he was following an antiphonary in which just such minor disarrangements had actually occurred
since the time of Gregory the Great. But it seems equally probable that
since he has intercalated two of the "additional O's" between pairs of the
"Great O's," he was following an order dictated, in part at least, by the
content of the antiphons.

At a somewhat later period Peter Comestor (CXCVIII.1737–38),
ruminating upon these "Major Antiphons," was able to imagine a progression in the concluding, imperative phrases, "in which the longing
and ardor of those who are waiting [for the Advent] is clearly revealed."
In the first, knowledge is requested, whose light will enlighten the darkness
of the threefold ignorance of man: ignorance of God, of himself, and of
virtue. The second petitions release from a triple servitude: of the devil,
of sin, and of debt. The third requests redemption; the fourth asks to be let
out of the prison of the Inferno; the fifth seeks illumination by the grace
of the Holy Spirit; while the last two look for salvation, that His spirit
may invest us while we are in this mortal flesh, so that at the final Judgment we shall find a place at the right hand of Him, "qui veniet judicare
vivos et mortuos et saeculum per ignem." This interpretative order, not
precisely the Gregorian, demonstrates how the antiphons could be adjusted
to a kind of spiritual chronology and shaped imaginatively in terms of one
component, their concluding petitions.

The strategy of the Old English poet is, of course, far more complex,
but like Comestor, he works with loosely formulated progressions woven
together in a fabric of considerable emotive and intellectual substance. He
uses the antiphonal petitions but gives them many voices—dramatic, historic, and personal—and associates them with related modes of spiritual
awareness. Throughout the sequence he maintains a sense of that inevitable
spiritual chronology which Comestor was to sketch out. But more conspicuously, he seizes upon the brilliant typological figures which dominate
these Advent antiphons and exploits and expands their visual and dramatic character. He explicates and expounds their doctrinal significance,
finding familiar meanings in new typological forms, or moving among
figuratively similar types, he injects new concepts or unusual emphases.
Thus his patterns of recurrence are formal, as the antiphonal shape is
reflected in each section, and figurative and doctrinal, as the types inter-
act, commingling tenors and vehicles.

Some such structural possibility was recognized by Campbell when he
spoke of "recurring ideas which appear from time to time like *leit motifs*,"
but he denied them any "observable pattern of thematic structure" (p. 10).

The kinds of progression the *Advent* provides are neither explicitly narrative nor discursive, yet there is certainly a structure to the poem which forbids us to call the order of the sections totally unimportant. Burgert, though he sought unity in a superficial and contrived "hymnic" structure, sensed the potential significance of typological patterns: "Scholars have found the frequent repetitions in the *Christ* one of the marring features of Cynewulf's poetry with disastrous effect upon the unity and orderly development of the plot. . . . In many cases . . . a closer examination might reveal new phases and new developments in the recurring theme" (p. 39n.) Burgert illustrates these structural possibilities in the tenth division, with such motifs as the coeternity of the Son with the Father, and the Christian soul as a captive in this world.

Stanley B. Greenfield, in his article "The Theme of Spiritual Exile in *Christ I,*" [8] proposed a far more elaborate analysis of the latter motif, maintaining in general that the poet has given a "logical and progressive development" to a series of images which evoke "the story of man's spiritual down-fall and subsequent exile." Greenfield considers that the dominant subject of the poem is "the goodness, grace and glory of Christ and the Virgin"; the dominant mood, one of joy. But against this is harmonized a "minor theme," "reflecting the Christian tradition of man's life as a spiritual exile from Heaven, Eden, and the natural bond with his Creator." This secondary motif, acting as the bass part in a musical composition, comments upon the "necessity for and meaning of Christ's Incarnation."

The first occurrence of the exile theme is in the second division, the *Clavis David,* where the prisoners in limbo are depicted awaiting in darkness the enlightenment of Christ. Greenfield takes lines 30b–32:

> þe he to wuldre forlet,
> þa *we* heanlice   hweorfan sceoldan
> to þis enge lond,   eðle bescyrede,

as a clear reference to the expulsion from Eden and the first direct statement about the Fall of Man and the subsequent influence of Original Sin. When the exile theme recurs in the *Oriens* section, it is couched in similiar language, but the emphasis is upon the length of time that the prisoners have been deprived of the divine radiance. In the next division, the *Emmanuel* paraphrase, the temporal element is given an immediacy by the fact that the petition is presented in direct address: there is a suggestion that the historical occasion of the first Advent is imminent. In the eighth section, *O Rex pacifice,* the kind of exile is somewhat different.

8. *PQ, 32* (1953), 321–28.

The reference is to a period following the Crucifixion; the dominant image, that of a scattered flock. The last passage, in the tenth division, that of unknown origin, summarizes and echoes verbally the whole conception of spiritual exile in a general moral context. This is the exile which is symbolized in the Fall and its consequences, the exile of the spirit from God through sin. As Greenfield says, "this exile is entirely of the present, and it contains the sum of all previous phases of exile which have, in the order of their presentation, recapitulated the story of man's moral downfall and subsequent wandering in sin" (p. 327).

Though his chronology is anchored in a somewhat doubtful reading,[9] Greenfield has clearly performed a service in isolating one motif in the structure of the poem and showing the kind of progression it makes possible. Equally useful, perhaps, is the musical analogy in which he has loosely couched his analysis. There is a dominant theme or major subject—"the goodness, grace and glory of Christ and the Virgin"—to which a minor theme, the spiritual exile of mankind, provides the bass. The term "minor" is obviously used not merely in the sense of "secondary" but with full musical associations of, first, a plaintive mode and, secondly, an understood relation to the major key, which would permit harmony and ultimately seek resolution into the dominant tonality.

The analogy to music is extremely suggestive, though, of course, it cannot be pressed too strictly. Such designations as "bass" or "harmony" imply a temporal relationship which is admittedly impossible in a verbal, hence univocal, structure. If a musical theme is contrapuntally related to another, the two must be produced simultaneously; harmonic elements

9. Greenfield's reading of lines 30–32, following Cook and Krapp-Dobbie, necessitates a slight emendation (*þa we* for *þa þe,* 31a) and a somewhat unexpected use of *forlet:* "Make us worthy of this, whom He hath admitted into heavenly glory when we abjectly had to turn into this narrow land, deprived of our native home" (p. 323). The "clear reference" to the Expulsion from Eden disappears if we translate with Campbell: "May he make us worthy that he has admitted us to glory, those who miserable had to turn . . ." (pp. 48, 84). The allusion to the Redemption in the past tense may be felt inappropriate to the dramatic situation, which is one of intense anticipation. J. C. Pope has suggested, in discussion, that we take the phrase *to wuldre* adverbially and give *forlet* its common meaning: "Make us worthy of that which He gloriously forsook . . ." In any case, there is no need to tie the "exile theme" to a fixed temporal sequence beginning with the Fall of Man. The attempt is perilous in view of our ignorance of the opening of the poem.

For the adverbial use of the phrase *to wuldre,* see Fr. Klaeber, in *JEGP,* 4 (1902–03), 108, and line 57 of this poem.

must be written or received audibly at the same instant. Poetry, however, is single and sequential, and lacking the multitemporal structure of music, its "harmony" and "counterpoint" are necessarily metaphoric. But these distinctions need not totally undermine the analogy, because in a verbal situation the retentive powers of the mind compensate for the temporal lag by recalling, juxtaposing, and harmonizing those elements which appear to have an intellectual or emotional rapport. Thus, when a given subject recurs in a poem with verbal echoes of the previous statement, or when a different but related idea is introduced, the reader or listener will make an association, mentally unite the two, and recreate the formal pattern of the poem. The recognition of associated passages may be immediate and subconscious or it may come as a delayed, intellectual response. This temporal adjustment occurs inevitably whenever we encounter a verbal statement. It is the basis of our most elementary grammatical comprehension as well as our most sophisticated literary intuitions. It is, of course, what makes it possible to speak of "form" or "structure" in literature. Yet we are commonly given a narrative or discursive organization which provides a clear temporal orientation and which, in a naive reading, is accepted as final. Where such familiar guides are absent, we feel disoriented and find the sequences arbitrary, the order unimportant. It is here that the analogy to the nonreferential art of music proves most rewarding.

The analogy of poetry to music ought not to be unfamiliar to the modern critic. T. S. Eliot, in his lecture on *The Music of Poetry,*[10] has expressed very similar sentiments:

> I believe that the properties in which music concerns the poet most nearly, are the sense of rhythm and the sense of structure . . . The use of recurrent themes is as natural to poetry as to music. There are possibilities for verse which bear some analogy to the development of a theme by different groups of instruments; there are possibilities of transitions in a poem comparable to the different movements of a symphony or a quartet; there are possibilities of contrapuntal arrangement of subject-matter.

The titles of many Eliot poems, notably the *Four Quartets,* indicate that he was writing consciously in terms of a musical analogy, and critics have described his poetry as the "music of ideas" [11] or the "music of meaning . . . where word relates to word, phrase to phrase, and image to

10. W. P. Ker Memorial Lecture (Glasgow, 1942), p. 28.

11. I. A. Richards, "The Poetry of T. S. Eliot," in his *Principles of Literary Criticism* (New York, 1959), App. B, p. 293.

image." [12] For I. A. Richards the analogy accounts for the structural bewilderment of most early readers of Eliot's poems at:

> the unobtrusiveness, in some cases the absence, of any coherent intellectual thread upon which the items of the poem are strung. For the items are united by the accord, contrast, and interaction of their emotional effects, not by an intellectual scheme that analysis must work out. The value lies in the unified response which this interaction creates in the right reader. The only intellectual activity required takes place in the realization of the separate items. We can, of course, make a 'rationalisation' of the whole experience, as we can of any experience. If we do, we are adding something which does not belong to the poem. Such a logical scheme is, at best, a scaffolding that vanishes when the poem is constructed. But we have so built into our nervous systems a demand for intellectual coherence, even in poetry, that we find a difficulty in doing without it.[13]

The "ideas" of Eliot's "music," Richards continues, "are of all kinds, abstract and concrete, general and particular, and, like the musician's phrases, they are arranged, not that they may tell us something, but that their effects in us may combine into a coherent whole of feeling and attitude and produce a peculiar liberation of the will." [14] It is perhaps not pressing the comparison too far to suggest that the literary allusions of Eliot are comparable to the typological allusions in the Old English *Advent,* to which an informed audience might respond without the distraction of elaborate analysis or "working out." As the Grail myth of Miss Weston's essay gives to *The Waste Land* an apparent coherence of imagery and event, so the narrative and liturgy of the Advent season act as a stabilizing factor to the types and doctrines of the sequence. And as disillusionment and sterility lend a tonal unity to Eliot's five-part structure, so the awe and wonder of the recurrent *Eala's,* like the "O's" of admiration in the antiphons themselves, remind us of the cohesive lyric impulse of the Old English poem.

The *Advent,* then, is a large scale composition, built up of smaller quasi-independent units and organized upon "musical principles." The poem is a composite of many themes or motifs related to the Advent, its mysteries, its historical reality, its figures, and its theological significance. A theme may be stated in terms of a typological image, a dramatic event, or a doc-

12. Helen Gardner, *The Art of T. S. Eliot* (New York, 1950), p. 55.
13. Richards, *Principles,* pp. 289–90.
14. Ibid., p. 293.

trinal proposition. The selection of themes within each movement is in part imposed by the antiphonal source but is just as often a matter of the poet's discretion. The recurrence of themes is inherent in the sources themselves, but the poet has appropriated the liturgical "schema," independently adding to or eliminating the separate components of each antiphon. While these themes are unequal in importance and in treatment, they occur and recur throughout the poem in distinguishable variations. One theme may first be introduced in its fullest statement, then return merely in allusion and echo; another will emerge gradually, taking form slowly and achieving a complete realization only in its final appearance. This thematic material is woven together as in a symphonic composition, and transitions range from the abrupt, strong emergence of a new motif to a subtle, blending "segue" from one subject to another. Thematic recurrence allows for various kinds of "development," while what Eliot has called the "contrapuntal arrangement of subject matter" is achieved by the juxtaposition of passages of contrasting tone or presentation, as well as by the confrontation of typological figures which are unrelated in their concrete aspect, though "harmonized" in doctrinal significance.

The *Advent* is, if I am correct in my estimate, subtle and unexpected. It is in some ways as difficult and unnerving to the modern reader as is *The Waste Land.* In Eliot's poem, however, the effect is produced by deliberate design, while in the Old English work we find ourselves alienated by remoteness in time and a consequent alteration in sensibility, modes of religious thought, and ways of imagining. It should, then, be neither surprising nor distasteful to the modern reader to find that, like the uninitiated student approaching *The Waste Land,* he requires a considerable body of commentary to penetrate the typology and theology of a poem written over a millennium ago. And if the musical analogy is to be demonstrated, then a painstaking thematic analysis is the only method. If I have erred on the side of liberality in providing patristic witness to the poem's figures, it is because the material is generally unfamiliar, and since the poet's intention is often not unmistakably clear, it was felt better to indicate the range of possibilities from which the given interpretation was selected. One might also hope that these glimpses into the processes of the typological imagination are as helpful to the understanding of the procedure of the poem as a whole, as some of them are to the elucidation of specific passages.

3. COMMENTARY

Mas be cre
Que ges chans ancse
No val al comensamen
Tan com pois, can om l'enten.

Giraut de Bornelh

Glosynge is a glorious thyng, certeyn.

Chaucer

THE DIFFICULTIES OF ANY COMPLETE ANALYSIS OF THE *ADVENT* sequence are considerably heightened at the outset by its fragmentary condition. This is a situation, however, in which all hope need not be abandoned. Intelligent conjecture on the part of Burgert has given a clue to the content of the missing leaves. He has noted that the sources of the existing twelve divisions of the poem, taken collectively, present a lacuna similar to that of the poem itself: "The absence of three Great O's, of the *O Sapientia,* the *O Adonai,* and the *O Radix* finds no precedent in the history of the liturgy" (p. 49). Four parts of an inseparable septet are engaged in the extant portion of the poem. It seems, therefore, more than likely that the remaining antiphons had found their place in the lost verses. Moreover, the poem supplements the "Major Seven" with four "additional O's," while it is known that as many as five were commonly employed, bringing the number of O-antiphons to twelve. We must therefore reckon with the possibility, first mentioned by Cook (p. 73), that "the early part of the poem may have contained a variation upon the Gabriel antiphon," the fifth of these "added or monastic O's." Consequently, any part or parts of these four antiphons may well have been involved in the lost opening of the poem.

If one were to conjecture further as to the very beginning of the *Advent,* barring the possibility of a nonantiphonal preface, it would seem most probable that the initial lines contained a paraphrase of the *O Sapientia* antiphon. This "Major O," without exception from the earliest record, heads the list of the "Great Seven." The theme it suggests is one which will occur several times again in the poem: Christ, as the Wisdom of God, begotten of Him before all other Creation, of which the Son was Himself the Agent. It further presents the Second Person of the Trinity in His most magnificent and remote aspect: "attingens a fine usque ad finem, fortiter suaviterque disponens omnia." The other "Great O's," not incorporated in the extant text, *O Adonai* and *O Radix Jesse,* address Christ primarily as the great Ruler and Lawgiver, employing a more accessible earthly metaphor: "dux domus Israel, qui Moysi . . . in Sina legem dedisti," "super quem continebunt reges os suum, quem gentes deprecabuntur." This terrestrial conception of the Lord, as the supreme Jewish monarch, is emphasized in the *Emmanuel* antiphon and in its Old English paraphrase as well. Moreover, each of these two O's contains a prominent Christian symbol commonly associated with the Blessed Virgin and the Incarnation. The bush which in the sight of Moses burned but was not consumed is a popular allegory for the perpetual virginity of Mary, who conceived the Word by the Holy Spirit, yet remained without blemish. The Root of Jesse, also a familiar symbol, was equally pertinent to the Virgin, through whose parentage Christ became the culmination of the great line of Hebrew kings descending from David and his father, Jesse. It cannot be assumed that either of these symbols was developed in the Old English text, but each would have introduced subjects which are prominent in the extant poem.

This is perhaps equally true of the *Gabriel* antiphon, which epitomizes the historical event of the Annunciation—a scene which might have found its way into the poem in semidramatic form, preceding those depicting the interrogation of the citizens of Jerusalem and the dilemma of Joseph. This hypothetical paraphrase could also have made possible the introduction of such items as the name Emmanuel and the image of the closed gates of Paradise through which the Archangel passed. Each of these typological motifs is later exploited more or less fully. On the other hand, the Annunciation is so thoroughly treated in the "Passus" and in the *O mundi Domina* section that one wonders whether the enigmatic tenth division was not a substitute for this antiphon. The visit of the Archangel is not precisely a part of the Advent season but an event which could be recollected from the past at the approaching moment of birth. Furthermore, it is difficult to say whether such an antiphon could have been successfully handled so as not to spoil the concentration upon Christ and the Virgin, which guides the rest of the poem.

Of particular concern to these conjectures is the condition of the manuscript. If it is not assumed that the *Advent* was the first poem in the *Exeter Book*, the length of the poem cannot be estimated and any amount of this relevant material may well have been incorporated into the poem. But the *Advent*, from its theme, from its spirit of invocation and praise, and from its length, would appear to have been the perfect choice to initiate an anthology of predominantly religious works, in which the longer poems have been sorted out toward the front of the book, the shorter toward the

end. In this case, one would suspect that the poem had been copied onto
the first folios of a gathering beginning the *Codex*. Since the fragment is
contained in a gathering of seven folios, while the standard number seems
to have been eight, the missing portion of the *Advent* probably involved
either one additional folio or that and another complete gathering. But the
latter alternative would totally unbalance the structure that is evident in
the extant fragment. If, then, only one folio were missing, 46 lines of
script or approximately 70 verse lines must be accounted for. Since the
early divisions in the poem do not much exceed 20 or 30 lines, it is quite
conceivable that there was space for 3 major sections—the *Sapientia,
Adonai,* and *Radix Jesse*—as well as a few lines at the opening of the
Rex gentium paraphrase. This would bring the poem to about 500 lines,
divided into 15 sections and including all of the "Great O's of Advent"
and their rich typology.

Division 1

I.   . . . cyninge.

Ðu eart se weallstan   þe ða wyrhtan iu
wiðwurpon to weorce.   Wel þe geriseð
þæt þu heafod sie   healle mærre,
ond gesomnige   side weallas   5
fæste gefoge,   flint unbræcne,
þæt geond eorðb[yr]g eall   eagna gesihþe
wundrien to worlde.   Wuldres ealdor,
gesweotula nu þurh searocræft   þin sylfes weorc,
soðfæst, sigorbeorht,   ond sona forlæt   10
weall wið wealle.   Nu is þam weorce þearf
þæt se cræftga cume   ond se cyning sylfa,
ond þonne gebete—   nu gebrosnad is—
hus under hrofe.   He þæt hra gescop,
leomo læmena;   nu sceal liffrea   15
þone wergan heap   wraþum ahreddan,
earme from egsan,   swa he oft dyde.

I.   . . . king.

You are the wall-stone that the workers of old
Rejected from the work; it is [now] most fitting
That You be the head of that great hall
And bring together the vast walls,   5
Indestructible flint, in firm conjunction,
That throughout earth's cities, all those with eyes to see
May gaze for ever.   Prince of glory,
Disclose now with skill Your proper work,
Fast in truth, bright with victory, and at once let   10
The wall [unite] with wall.   Now there is need of such work:
That the Craftsman come, the King Himself,
And then restore—it is now in ruin—
The house beneath the roof.   He created the body,
The limbs of clay; now must the Lord of life   15
Release from the wrathful this weary throng,
These helpless from terror, as He often has.

O Rex gentium et desideratus earum, lapisque angularis qui facis utraque unum: veni, et salva hominem quem de limo formasti.

THE ANTIPHON OF THE MAGNIFICAT FOR DECEMBER 22 IS CLEARLY the source of the fragmentary section which opens the *Advent,* but the poet had equally in mind the psalmic text from which the "cornerstone" image was derived: "The stone which the builders rejected, has become the head of the corner [*caput anguli*]" (117:22). The recovery of the rejected stone, which symbolized a triumphant resolution to the longings of the Jewish people, became one of the most popular and fertile images in Christian typology. A Messianic prophecy to the later Jews, the text was interpreted in the Gospels and in Acts as a prefiguration of the crucified Savior. The most influential and effective use of the passage was, however, that of St. Paul in the Epistle to the Ephesians (2:20–22), where it is referred to the union in Christ of the Gentiles with the Jews, since through Him all have access in one Spirit to the Father. The uncircumcised have become part of the House of the Lord, "built upon the foundation of the Apostles and Prophets, Jesus Christ himself being the chief cornerstone [*ipso summo angulari lapide, Christo Jesu*]: In whom all the building is brought together and grows up into a holy temple in the Lord."

The Psalmist's phrase "caput anguli" is architecturally ambiguous but seems to mean "the front part or most forward part of an angle or corner." [1] Whereas some modern commentators have understood the biblical reference as "one of the four highest cornerstones or, more probably, as the last stone laid in the building of an edifice,—more exactly as the coping stone above a portal," [2] G. B. Ladner has shown that in early medieval exegesis the symbolism is "pre-eminently that of a corner-stone of the foundations." [3] The later confusion arises most probably from St. Paul's

1. Gerhart B. Ladner, "The Symbolism of the Biblical Corner Stone in the Mediaeval West," *MS, 4* (1942), 43–60; see p. 45.
2. Ibid., p. 44.
3. Ibid., p. 48.

imagery, when in two sequential passages he speaks first of a "wall" (2:14) and then of the "foundations" and "chief corner-stone" of the temple (2:20). The wall, which in Paul's text is the former enmity of the Gentiles and Jews, now broken down by Christ ("medium parietem maceriae solvens"), is taken into the temple image, where Christ as the cornerstone unites the two peoples, now two walls. In exegetical usage it is not always clear, however, whether we are to see the joining stone in the foundation or at the top of the walls.

Nor is the Old English text quite unambiguous. The poet takes over the patristic image in some detail. The rejected stone is to bring together the walls and be the head of the great hall (2–4). The use of *heafod* is perhaps an elliptical reference to the "caput anguli" but is also meant to suggest the image of the Church as a living body of which Christ is the head. In any case, the Old English text seems to suggest an elevated cornerstone rather than one at the foundation of the joined walls. There is some early evidence for such a view. Tertullian (II.330), at the end of the second century, refers to the "chief cornerstone, taken up after its rejection, and raised on high [*sublimatus*] for the completion of the temple, which is, of course, the Church." And St. Maximus of Turin (LVII.821) anticipates lines 3b–4 of our poem with the additional words: "Deservedly it is at the head, for He Himself is the head of the Church as well as the foundation." Christ is both above and below, being both God and man, Word and flesh. However the *Advent* poet visualized the cornerstone image, his allusive phrasing, *heafod healle mærre,* clearly points to an interpretation of the figure as one for the founding of the universal Church.

Indeed, any other explanation would have been most surprising, since the early Fathers are unanimous in following the Pauline typology. Only in the elaboration is there some divergence. The role of the "aedificantes" is consistently assigned to the agents of the Crucifixion, who, according to pseudo-Bede (XCIII.1051), sought to establish their own justice and not to be subjected to that of God. They rejected the Savior, preferring instead an earthly king. Arnobius Junior (LIII.505), developing the figurative plot, explains that those who rejected the stone were seeking a stone for one wall only, whereas this stone must serve for two, as God proved by placing it at the head of the angle, that it might unite two walls, two testaments, two peoples. The antiphonal phrase, "qui facis utraque unum," occurs in the Ephesians passage, preceding by only a few lines the image of the "cornerstone," and the two texts are regularly found together in much patristic exegesis, as in the antiphon, with a consistent interpretation. Cook (p. 75) cites the gloss in the *Moralia* of Gregory the Great as typical and perhaps influential upon the Anglo-Saxon Church: "Now it is clear to all through divine grace that when He, Whom holy Scripture calls the cornerstone, takes unto Himself the Jews on the one side and the Gentiles on the other, He joins as it were the two walls in the one building of the Church" (LXXVI.458–59).

Cook further suggests that there was a second common interpretation of "qui fecit utraque unum," referring to the reconciliation of the Church on earth and the angels in heaven. This reading of the image stems from the association of yet another passage from Ephesians. Paul, in the first chapter, explains that by the Redemption, God's hidden purpose is made known: "in the fullness of time to restore in Christ all things that are in heaven and on earth, in Him" (1:10). This explication of the conjunction brought about by the angle stone (Christ) of the two walls (men and angels) takes second place among the Fathers to the one explicitly given by Paul, but it is found in the writings of such significant exegetes as Jerome (XXVI.476) and Gregory (LXXVI.459), and most importantly for an Old English text, in Bede. In a homily for Palm Sunday (XCIV.124) the Anglo-Saxon saint follows the traditional explanation— the union of Gentile and Jew, an action accomplished historically in the founding of the Church—with an eschatological reading: Christ's advent was not only to man on earth but also to the angels, whose numbers in heaven the fall of Satan had diminished and were to be replenished by those He had come to redeem. In another context (XCI.853) Paul's image of the temple, "habitaculum Dei in Spiritu" (2:22), which is the spiritual Church, the whole congregation of the elect, angels and men, is seen to be prefigured in the temple of Solomon and in Jerusalem, which in its celestial aspect is a vision of "pax nostra, qui fecit utraque unum." That pacific state is the true Church, united by Christ the Redeemer, "Who dissolved the enmity between God and man in His own flesh." [4]

These typological connections, of great importance to the *Advent* sequence, are found again in the homilies of Ælfric, which Cook (pp. 75–76) rightly cites as useful analogues to the Old English poem. Ælfric, like Bede, alludes to both interpretations of the "lapis angularis." The primary one is found in a sermon on the Epiphany, as a comment on the Psalmist's text, and is of interest for the way in which it expands the architectural image in terms like those of the *Advent* poet:

Soðlice se sealm-sceop awrat be Criste, þæt he is se hyrn-stan þe gefegð
þa twegen weallas togædere, forðan ðe he geþeodde his gecorenan of

4. See also the sermons collected among the doubtful works of Augustine (XXXIX.2171) and Maximus of Turin (LVII.884).

Iudeiscum folce and þa geleaffullan of hæðenum, swilce twegen wagas to anre gelaðunge.

[For the psalmist wrote concerning Christ, that he is the corner-stone which joins the two walls together, because he united his chosen of the Jewish people and the faithful of the heathen, as two walls, to one church.] [5]

The secondary interpretation is not related to the cornerstone image specifically. It glosses the "utraque unum" of Ephesians 2:14, "þæt is, engla werod and mancynn to anum werode." [6] This homily was written for the dedication of a church and is mostly taken up with the story of the building of Solomon's temple and its typological reference.[7] Ælfric tells how God's gift of wisdom to the King brought about a great prosperity which made possible the magnificent structure. It does not suit his purpose to allude to the rejected cornerstone as a part of the story of Solomon's effort, but his figurative explanation of the "templum Dei" indicates clearly that he was familiar with it in this connection:

Se gesibsuma Salomon arærde þæt mære hus of eorðlicum antimbre Gode to wurðmynte, and se gesibsuma Crist getimbrode ða gastlican cyrcan, na mid deadum stanum, ac mid lybbendum sawlum, swa swa se apostol Petrus awrat to geleaffulre gelaðunge: he cwæð, "Genealæcað to ðam lybbendum stane, seðe is fram mannum aworpen, and fram Gode gecoren and gearwurðod; and beoð ge sylfe ofer ðam stane getimbrode, swa swa lybbende stanas on gastlicum husum." Crist is se lybbenda stan þone awurpon ða ungeleaffullan Iudei; ac se Heofenlica Fæder hine geceas æfter ðære menniscnysse, and gearwurðode, swa þæt he hylt ealle ða gebytlu ðære geleaffullan gelaðunge. Ealle Godes cyrcan sind getealde to anre cyrcan, and seo is gehaten "gelaðung," ða getacnode þæt an tempel ðe Salomon arærde on ðære ealdan æ.

[The peaceful Solomon reared the great house of earthly material to the honour of God, and the peaceful Christ constructed the ghostly church,

5. Benjamin Thorpe, ed., *The Homilies of Ælfric, 1* (2 vols. London, 1844–46), 106–07; Thorpe's trans.

6. "That is, the host of angels and mankind to one host," *Homilies, 2,* 580–81.

7. I am grateful to J. C. Pope for pointing out to me the source of this homily in Bede's *De Templo Salomonis,* chaps. 1 and 2 (XCI.737–39), and in a pseudo-Augustinian sermon (XXXIX.2171–72), also attributed to Maximus of Turin (LVII.883–86) and cited in n. 3, above.

not with dead stones, but with living souls, as the apostle Peter wrote to the faithful church: he said, "Draw near unto the living stone, which is rejected of men, and chosen of God and honoured; and ye yourselves shall be built on that stone, as living stones in ghostly houses." Christ is the living stone that the unbelieving Jews rejected; but the Heavenly Father chose and honoured him after his humanity, so that he holds together all the buildings of the faithful church. All God's churches are accounted as one church, and that is called *congregation,* which was betokened by that one temple that Solomon reared in the old law.] [8]

Ælfric's interpretation of the images of Solomon's house and the stones of which it was constructed is of considerable importance for our understanding of the opening section of the *Advent* sequence. First, it testifies to the currency in Anglo-Saxon times of the story of the "rejected stone," and second, it provides in the same context a classic statement of the figure of the "house" composed of living stones.

The primary source for the legend of the building of Solomon's temple is the apocryphal literature ascribed to the great King, in particular, that encyclopedia of demonology, *The Testament of Solomon.* By virtue of the pentalpha ring, Solomon gains power over the chief of the demons, Beelzeboul, and his unholy crew, who are then assigned tasks in the building of the temple. The work is completed by them except for "a stone, the end stone of the corner lying there, great, chosen out, one which I desired to lay in the head of the corner of the completion of the Temple." [9] The stone was "exceedingly great and useful," but all of the workmen with all of the demons helping them were unable to stir it. The dilemma is solved by a spirit of the winds named Ephippas of Arabia, who, though confined in a flask, "went up the steps, carrying the stone, and laid it down at the entrance of the Temple." Solomon declares that the Scripture is fulfilled and cites the "cornerstone" verse of the Psalm. God in His mysterious ways has brought about the completion of the Temple. [10]

That some such folk tale, involving the cornerstone text with the Temple of Solomon, persisted during the first Christian millennium is confirmed by the association of ideas in Ælfric's homily and by their firm rejection in

8. *Homilies, 2,* 580–81.

9. I quote from the translation of F. C. Conybeare in the *Jewish Quarterly Review, 11* (1899), 41–43.

10. A similar incident occurs in the 5th-century life of the Georgian St. Nino, translated by Marjory and Oliver Wardrop in *Studia Biblica et Ecclesiastica,* V, No. 1, (Oxford, 1900).

the writings of St. Bruno the Carthusian (CLII.1254): "The story that during the building of Solomon's Temple, one stone was rejected by the builders and at the very last was placed in the corner, seems to be a complete falsehood, since it is not found in any history." One can only guess at the form which the legend took during those years, but it was undoubtedly less elaborate than the tale which appears in the early fourteenth-century compendium of typology, the *Speculum humanae salvationis*,[11] where it appears as the third figure for the Resurrection, complete with the traditional exegesis of the walls as the Jews and Gentiles united in one Church, and with the additional flourish of the mortar and stone representing the blood and body of the Lord.

One need not have lingered so long over this fanciful tale were it not that the *Advent* is permeated with related architectural figures—cities, temples, stones, walls, gates, doors, and keys. The first full line of the poem begins abruptly: *Ðu eart se weallstan.* The phrase is structurally similar to that of line 328: *þu eart þæt wealldor,* where the announced figure is preceded by thirty lines of description in which it is elaborately anticipated. The first leaf of the manuscript plunges into the middle of the *O Rex gentium* paraphrase, leaving an isolated word, *cyninge,* before the first complete verse. Cook (p. 73) assumes that "here the reference must be to the 'Rex' of the Antiphon," because, with a single exception in this poem (line 165), *cyning* always denotes God or Christ. It seems unlikely that at this point in the poem any antecedent portion of the Temple narrative would have been inserted in the paraphrase, as it is in the later section *O mundi Domina,* where it occurs independent of antiphonal inspiration. Probably the poet began his paraphrase with an epithet other than "King" and approached the opening words of the antiphon obliquely, as he does in the second division. The dative *cyninge* could be part of a free rendering of the phrase "desideratus earum": "the nations desired Him for their King." Perhaps *cyninge* was the second member of a compound such as *þeodcyninge* or *heahcyninge*.[12] However we reconstruct the missing portion of this section, it is clear from what follows that the poet knew the "story" of the construction of the Temple and the rejected stone. It would be impossible to argue that he knew anything like the apocryphal legend, but Bede's treatise, *De Templo Salomonis* (XCI.735–808) and Ælfric's ser-

11. See the edition of J. Lutz and P. Perdrizet, (Mülhausen, 1907–09), p. 67. An English translation of the 15th century was privately printed for the Roxburghe Club, *The Miroure of Mans Salvacionne* (London, 1888), see pp. 113–14.

12. I owe these textual suggestions to J. C. Pope.

mon prove that a detailed typological analysis of that edifice was not unfamiliar to the Anglo-Saxon church.

The striking thing about the *Advent* poet's treatment of the figure is the oblique, characteristically typological approach, which allows for a multiplicity of meanings. The chief aspects of the event—Christ as the cornerstone, rejected, then elevated—are directly expressed in the opening lines:

Ðu eart se weallstan   þe ða wyrhtan iu
wiðwurpon to weorce.   Wel þe geriseð
þæt þu heafod sie   healle mærre,
ond gesomnige   side weallas.   (2–5)

But there is no explicit interpretation of the hall or its two walls. The words *healle mærre* certainly suggest a temple or church, as Cook (p. 74) had proposed, and the association of *heafod* with the Pauline image of the spiritual body of Christ (I Cor. 12) would more than likely have summoned up, for the ecclesiastically educated reader, the idea of the universal Church. Perhaps this interpretation is also intended in the lines:

ond þonne gebete—   nu gebrosnad is—[13]
hus under hrofe,   (13–14a)

where the state of severe disrepair may signify a communal slackening of faith, humanity in a condition of sin, seeking restoration in the Advent of Christ. *Hus,* we recall, is Ælfric's term for the Temple of Solomon, a figure for the Church of Christ.

Cook (p. 75) states that Ælfric recognized two senses in the metaphor of the *hus,* "the one church universal" and "the individual Christian," but no distinction is typologically necessary. The Church of Ælfric's text is a spiritual entity, composed of "living stones," its individual members. The building whose walls were joined by Christ the "Cornerstone" and must now be restored by the same Agent, is not to be limited by its physical representation, no matter how graphic the imagery. Even lines 7–8, which refer to sensory perception, must be taken in a spiritual sense. Their source is also Psalm 117, and the line (23) follows directly upon the "lapis angularis" passage as in our poem: "And it is wonderful in our eyes." St. Augustine's gloss upon the visual image (XXXVII. 1499) is most pertinent to the Old English context: "With the eyes of the inner man, with the

---

13. The house in disrepair may be a confused recollection of Paul's image of the "broken middle wall of partition" (Eph. 2:14). The figure is there a positive one; the wall is the enmity between Gentiles and Jews, and the agent of destruction is Christ.

eyes of believers, of those who hope and love; not with the bodily eyes of those who have rejected the Man, as it were by despising Him." What is seen with the spiritual eye is the living Church. A distinction between the individual and the body of the universal Church is typologically negligible and obscures the coherence of this section. Metaphorically they are one, sharing a common tenor; spiritually and historically they are coincident. The establishment of the Church was manifest in the founding of individual faith; and the reconstruction of the former depends upon the restoration of the latter.

The paraphrase of the antiphonal petition with which this division concludes merely confirms the multiple significance of its typological figure:

> He þæt hra gescop,
> leomo læmena; [14]   nu sceal liffrea
> þone wergan heap   wraþum ahreddan,
> earme from egsan,   swa he oft dyde.   (14b–17)

The individual body of man is not to be dissociated from the figure of the Church. The alliteration of the monosyllables *hra* and *hus* emphasizes the spiritual identity of the living Church and the living man, and the theological unity of Creation and Redemption in the single Agent. The poet moves from the Church, *hus,* to the created individual, *hra,* to the composite body, *heap,* with no apparent disjunction of reference, and the central image of building and reconstruction applies equally to each, for the ultimate significance of one is inseparable from that of the other. The reduplication of figural referents is an illusion which the typological imagination dispels, for it, like the Redeemer, "facit utraque unum."

Thus, in this first fragmentary movement of the extant poem, we have a symbol of great prominence, manifesting the permanent function of Christ in a Christian world, the Head of the universal Church, the very Power which holds the edifice together. He is both the Creator and *se Cræftga,* the Craftsman who builds and redeems. There is a permanent need of His Coming, for the "house" is constantly in need of repair and threatening to collapse. As the Savior of mankind not once but repeatedly, *swa he oft dyde* (17b), Christ comes to man in a perpetual advent, to which the liturgical season gives form and timely reminder. This powerful image of the Creator is a theme which may have been announced in still more lofty terms in an earlier paraphrase of the *Sapientia* antiphon: "at-

14. Compare Ælfric's translation of Paul: "Nyte ge þæt eowere lima syndon þæs Halgan Gastes temple, seðe on eow is?" ("Know ye not that your limbs are the temple of the Holy Ghost, who is in you?"), *Homilies, 2,* 580–81.

tingens a fine usque ad finem fortiter, suaviter, disponensque omnia."
Against this expansive motif is set in humble counterpoint the frail figure
of mankind broken in sin, the wretched flock oppressed by a hostile foe.
The petitioners associate their created bodies with the spiritual body of
Christ, the Church, of which they are the humble but living stones. In the
plea for redemption they reinterpret the antiphonal phrase, "qui facis
utraque unum," seeking reconciliation between God and man, and the restoration of the spiritual Church, the temple of the Lord, the celestial
Jerusalem. This contrapuntal statement and the variations upon these resonant themes, as yet only implicit, will seek full development as the poem
progresses.

Division II

II. Eala þu reccend   ond þu riht cyning,
se þe locan healdeð,   lif ontyneð,
eadga[n] upwegas,   oþrum forwyrneð   20
wlitigan wilsiþes,   gif his weorc ne deag.
Huru we for þearfe   þas word sprecað,
and m[ynd]giað   þone þe mon gescop
þæt he ne [læ]te   [to l]ose weorðan
cearfulra þing,   þe we in carcerne   25
sittað sorgende,   sunnan wenað,°
hwonne us liffrea   leoht ontyne,
weorðe ussum mode   to mundboran,
ond þæt tydre gewitt   tire bewinde,
gedo usic þæs wyrðe,   þe he to wuldre forlet—   30
þa þe heanlice   hweorfan sceoldan
to þis enge lond,   eðle bescyrede.

   Forþon secgan mæg,   se ðe soð spriceð,
þæt he ahredde,   þa forhwyrfed wæs,
frumcyn fira.   Wæs seo fæmne geong,   35
mægð manes leas,   þe he him to meder geceas;
þæt wæs geworden   butan weres frigum,
þæt þurh bearnes gebyrd   bryd eacen wearð.
Nænig efenlic þam,   ær ne siþþan,
in worlde gewearð   wifes gea[c]nung; °   40
þæt degol wæs,   dryhtnes geryne.
Eal giofu gæstlic   grundsceat geondspreot;
þær wisna fela   wearð inlihted,
lare longsume,   þurh lifes fruman
þe ær under hoðman   biholen lægon,   45
witgena woðsong,   þa se waldend cwom,
se þe reorda gehwæs   ryne gemiclað
ðara þe geneahhe   noman scyppendes
þurh horscne had   hergan willað.

II. You, O Ruler and rightful King,
Who guard the lock, Who open life,
The blessed ways to heaven, [yet] withhold from another   20
That bright, longed-for journey, if his work does not merit.
Out of great need we speak these words
And are mindful of Him who created man
So that He may not allow to be lost utterly
This cause of the care-laden, for which we in prison   25
Sit sorrowing and wait for the sun,
That the Lord of life may open light upon us
And become to our spirit a protector,
The weak understanding encompass with grace,
And make us worthy of that which He gloriously forsook—   30
We who abjectly were forced to turn
To this narrow land, cut off from home.
    For indeed one may say who speaks truth
That He delivered, when it had turned aside,
That primal race of man. The woman was young,   35
A guiltless virgin, whom He chose as mother;
It was accomplished without a man's embrace
That, conceiving a child, the bride became great.
Nothing like to this, before or since,
Has happened in the world, this pregnancy in woman;   40
It was obscure, a mystery of the Lord.
All spiritual gifts sprouted forth throughout the earth;
There many a shoot was brought to light
Through the Giver of life—lasting doctrines
Which before lay covered under the dark earth,   45
Songs of the prophets—when the Ruler came,
Who magnifies the course of every word
Of those who earnestly wish to praise
With wisdom the name of the Creator.

O Clavis David, et sceptrum domus Israel, qui aperis et nemo claudit, claudis et nemo aperit, veni et educ vinctum de domo carceris, sedentem in tenebris, et umbra mortis.

INDEED, THE DEVELOPMENT OF THE MAJOR CONTRAPUNTAL themes of the first division seems to be the immediate concern of the second. As in the antiphonal sources, there is a powerful contrast between the activities of the almighty Lord and the plaintive passivity of dependent mankind. But there are equally apparent differences. The figure for Christ receives nothing like the elaboration of the cornerstone image; in fact, the "clavis David" almost disappears from view. In contrast, however, the voice of the petitioners, the *wergan heap,* is given a striking dramatic context in accord with the final phrases of the antiphon depicting the "captives of the prison house sitting in darkness and the shadow of death." Though we need not follow Greenfield in finding an allusion to the Fall from Eden and hence the beginning of a precise temporal sequence,[1] the theme of "spiritual exile" is indisputably stated here, though not necessarily for the first time. The motif is realized in terms of the Patriarchs and Prophets, confined to hell and waiting for the Advent of Christ.[2] We may observe that the statement grows not only out of the antiphonal phrases but also from the reference at the conclusion of the previous division (16–17) to mankind as a body, "a weary multitude," suffering enmity and terror. What was there merely the laconically expressed object of divine Redemption is now given a dramatic voice, which absorbs the vocative portion of the antiphon and endows the figures for the Redeemer with an unusual fluidity.

The typology of the first division is not abandoned, however. The royal titles which permeate the "Great O's" are given precedence in the opening line, *Eala þu reccend ond þu riht cyning,* echoing *se cyning sylfa* of line 12. And the role of Creator is again alluded to, though incidentally, in line 23b: *þone þe mon gescop.* But the striking figure by which the antiphonal

1. See above, p. 47, n. 9.
2. See Cook's discussion, *Christ,* pp. 79–80.

source of this division is identified is surprisingly underplayed. It is, in fact, uncertain that the "key" actually occurs in the Old English text. "Some of the finest things in the Latin text," Campbell has rightly asserted, "such as the neat rhetorical repetition and reversal in the doctrine section, apparently did not interest the poet at all" (p. 13). The typological associations of the figure were not, however, far from the poet's mind.

The "Key of David" has a scriptural source in each Testament. In the twenty-second chapter of Isaiah the Lord invests Eliachim with the stewardship of the house of Judah, the inhabitants of Jerusalem. In token of this honor He promises to place "clavem domus David super humerum ejus" (22:22). The power of the keys was given by the king to his "housemayor," and since the actual keys were long and heavy and commonly worn over the shoulder, the investiture was, more often than not, symbolic. The position was of the highest authority, for it implied not only access to the house and all of its apartments but the right to admit and to refuse admission to the royal presence. In the Apocalypse (3:7) the symbol recurs, again in the language of the antiphon, though here it is "Sanctus et Verus" who possesses the keys. In the letter to the Church at Philadelphia the Lord proclaims His New Jerusalem, which is open to the Gentiles who have kept His word and not denied His name, but it is closed to those who have lied in calling themselves Jews, while denying the true Messiah. Like Eliachim in the old house of David, the earthly Jerusalem, Christ carries the keys of the new city of David, the kingdom of God.

Clearly, then, the "clavis David" can be seen as a refinement of the "lapis angularis" figure of the preceding division, continuing superficially the architectural metaphor, while theologically expanding the implications of the Redemption. The universal Church, of which Christ is the "cornerstone" and which is composed of both Jew and Gentile, is now viewed under its eternal aspect. The believers are separated from the "false Jews" of the "synagogue of Satan," those who denied the name of the Lord; and the "key" opens the way to eternal life or death. This extension of the figure is tied to two other New Testament passages: "I have the keys of death and of hell," says the Lord (Apoc. 1:18), and in the most famous text concerning the founding of the Church, Jesus says to His disciple, "Thou art Peter, and upon this rock [*petram*] I will build my church, and the gates of hell shall not prevail against it. And I will give to thee the keys of the kingdom of heaven" (Matt. 16:18–19). Thus, just as, with the "rock" and the "cornerstone," the Church on earth is united, with the "key" the Church eternal is divided from the infernal regions of the damned.

Surprisingly, this interpretation of the "clavis David" was not a common one in the first millennium, though a few writers come quite close to it. Alcuin (C.1111) and Haymo (CXVII.989), for example, explain the figure as the "incarnatio Christi," the Redeemer Himself being the door ("I am the door," John 10:9), the access for mankind to God and eternal life. Previously this door had been closed to all except the Prophets and Patriarchs, who, through the grace of the Holy Spirit, recognized His Advent. But with the Incarnation it is opened to all believers, closed to all infidels. These associations were clearly in the mind of the Old English poet as well, and he follows the scriptural understanding of the "key" figure when he joins alliteratively the *loca* with *lif*. It is the "righteous King [the Key], Who guards the lock,[3] Who opens [eternal] life":

> se þe locan healdeð,   lif ontyneð
> eadgan upwegas,   oþrum forwyrneð
> wlitigan wilsiþes,   gif his weorc ne deag.   (19–21)

To recapitulate briefly, the strategy of this second division of the *Advent* reverses that of the first, giving dramatic prominence to the voice and situation of the petitioners and subduing the visual and concrete aspect of the Christian figure. One might almost say that the setting of the petition, the "domus carceris," becomes the central image, while the contrapuntal theme varies disconcertingly. We have seen how the concepts of Christ as the Creator of Man and as Redeemer of the Church lead to the figure of the divine Judge, Who determines admission to the Messianic Kingdom. Though the theology is not entirely inexplicit, this movement of thought is accomplished primarily through the typological motifs, from the "rejected Cornerstone" to the "Key of David."

But the "Key" is not the only figure for Christ in these sections. Out of the darkness of the prison-house setting rises the image of light,[4] the "Sun," for which the Patriarchs and Prophets wait sorrowing. The "light" which they hope for is the light of heavenly glory, of salvation and eternal life, as the echo of *lif ontyneð* (19b) in *leoht ontyne* (27b) suggests. But the Sun is also the "Sun of Righteousness," and the expected reward of "light" is related to the judicial aspects of the "Key" motif in a transitional passage:

> þæt he ne [læ]te   [to l]ose weorðan
> cearfulra þing,   (24–25a)

---

3. I follow the reading of Stanley B. Greenfield in his note, "Of Locks and Keys—Line 19a of the Old English *Christ*," *MLN*, 67 (1952), 238–40.

4. The "light" motif is perhaps touched upon in line 10: *sigorbeorht*.

"that He may not allow to come to destruction this cause of the care-full."

It is the figure of "light" which prepares for the second part of this division (33–49), where the theme will be the mysterious "illumination" of divine prophecy. One plea in the petition of those who dwell in darkness is that the light may be as a protection to their spirits and *þæt tydre gewitt tire bewinde* (29). The second half begins with a flat assertion of illumined truth, an article of faith:

> Forþon secgan mæg,   se ðe soð spriceð,
> þæt he ahredde,   þa forhwyrfed wæs,
> frumcyn fira. (33–35a)

The word *ahredde* recalls its occurrence at the end of the first division (16), where salvation was merely a distressing need. In the first part of this section it was an expectation for which one begged to be made worthy. Now it is spoken of as an accomplished fact. But in the explanation which follows, we are not taken farther in the historical chronology of events than the pregnancy of Mary. That she conceived without the agency of man is, we are told, a dark mystery of the Lord: *þæt degol wæs, dryhtnes geryne* (41). This is another meaning of the "darkness" of the prison in which the Prophets dwelt, a darkness which is also "illuminated" (*wearð inlihted,* 43b) by the coming of Christ.

At this point, as Campbell has nicely demonstrated (p. 15), the metaphoric structure shifts again, and the image of the "light of the sun" is directed toward the darkness of the earth, from which sprout the spiritual gifts, the songs of the Prophets, which have long lain hidden beneath the earth. The combination of natural growth and the divine agency of conception, emphasized in the declaration of Mary's pregnancy,[5] is now repeated in relation to the prophecies of that event. Campbell's reading of *wisna fela* (43a) as "many a shoot"[6] makes clear the organic metaphor by which the poet has completed the analogy. This interpretation has considerable scriptural support. The line, *Eal giofu gæstlic grundsceat geond-spreot* (42), is doubtless dependent upon the plant image of the famous prophecy in Isaiah 11:1, "the sprout [*virga*] from the root of Jesse," which is followed immediately by a catalogue of what became known as the "Gifts of the Holy Spirit." The figure of a tree of spiritual Gifts is developed fre-

5. All the more emphatic if we accept the emendation of MS. *gearnung* to *geacnung* (40b). See Cook, *Christ,* p. 81.

6. The accepted translation has been "many a thing" (Gollancz) or "many matters; many hints" (see Cook's glossary).

quently and extensively by medieval exegetes,[7] taking many forms from the "tree of Jesse" to the "tree of virtues," for which, according to Hugh of St. Victor (CLXXVI.114), the Gifts of the Spirit provide the seeds, planted in the earth of the human heart. The connection between the spiritual Gifts and the words of the Prophets, made by the *Advent* poet, is, however, probably indebted to another passage in Isaiah. It is the Lord speaking:

> As the rain and the snow come down from heaven, and return not thither, but water the earth, making it bring forth and sprout, giving seed to the sower and bread to the eater,
> So shall my word be that goes forth from my mouth; it shall not return to me empty, but it shall accomplish that which I purpose, and prosper the thing for which I sent it. (55:10–11)

In traditional exegeses of this passage the "word" is usually taken to be the "Verbum Dei Patris," the incarnate Lord Himself, but it is applied equally to "evangelical doctrine," the words of the Apostles, by which Christian faith was diffused throughout the earth.[8] From such an interpretation it would have been an easy step for the *Advent* poet to include the teachings of the Prophets [9] among those numerous verbal shoots, nurtured by the moisture of the divine Word, or, as he puts it, irradiated by the divine Sun. In any case, the poet in this remarkably compressed passage is extending in terms of organic growth the concept of divine intervention into human history—literally, as the Word became flesh in the womb of Mary, and metaphorically, as the grace of the Holy Spirit took root in the visions of the Prophets and sprouted forth in the *witgena woðsong*.

The section ends with a description of the *Waldend* which comprehends all that has gone before:

> se þe reorda gehwæs   ryne gemiclað
> ðara þe geneahhe   noman scyppendes
> þurh horscne had   hergan willað.   (47–49)

7. See Rosemond Tuve, *Allegorical Imagery* (Princeton, 1966), p. 109 and note; and Eleanor Simmons Greenhill, "The Child in the Tree," *Traditio, 10* (1954), 323–71.

8. See Jerome (XXIV.556) and Haymo (CXVI.1005).

9. The closest patristic source I have found is Cassiodorus' exposition of Psalm 79:10 (LXX.582): "You planted the roots [of the vineyard], and it filled the land." "Its roots," he says, "are the prophets, implanted by the operation of the King of heaven. From these, the earth shooting forth small, happy sprouts, seems to fill up the whole world as if with pleasant shady bowers of faith."

In these lines we are reminded of the many ways in which the two halves of this section are bound together. The Prophets of the second part, who spoke mysteriously and whose prophecies were illuminated by the mystery of the Virgin Birth, are those Prophets of the first part who waited in the infernal prison for the illumination of the righteous Sun. And, of all those who lived historically before the Advent, it is only they who, in their prophetic wisdom, were granted the gift of expectation and the desire to be worthy. It was only they who then knew to praise the name of the Lord with wisdom.

As fully as the dramatic situation of the imprisoned Prophets, the typological figure of the "Key of David" runs through and binds together both halves of this section. In the first part, as we have seen, the interpretation centered upon the gift of eternal life, which was opened to those whose works availed, who believed and did not deny the name of the Lord. But it has already been mentioned that this was not the common patristic reading of the figure. One meaning of "clavis domus David," put forward by Haymo (CXVI.823) in the ninth century and later by Hervaeus (CLXXXI.219), was "scientia Scripturarum" or "scientia interpretandi Scripturas"—that is, the science of typology itself, opened by the Lord to His disciples and through them to the entire Church. Another exegete, Berengaud (XVII.788) explains the passage in Revelation in this fashion: "The Son of God possesses the key of David, because He Himself took on manhood out of the line of David. This manhood He calls the key of David, by which all things have been unlocked—both what God told to David, and what David spoke about Him." The Old Testament was opened to the knowledge of the divine mystery, and this none may close. Primasius (LXVIII.810), known to the Anglo-Saxons through Bede (XCIII.141), who cribbed extensively from him, transmitted a similar reading of the passage. David was not only a parent, but also a type of Christ, through Whom the writings of David as well as the law of Moses were opened: "All things must needs be fulfilled, which are written in the law of Moses and in the prophets and in the psalms concerning me" (Luke 24:44). Through the power of Christ, the secrets of the divine law are open to the faithful and closed to unbelievers, for the door which yields to the key of David is the Church: "The door which Christ opens, began then to be unlocked for the Church, when He opened to His disciples the [hidden] sense that they might understand the Scriptures."

Thus the two interpretations of the "clavis David" correspond to the two halves of the section of the Old English poem, which uses the antiphon for its source. Beginning with the notion of the "key to eternal life," an extension of the architectural image for the Church in the preceding section, the poet turns to the "key of the Scriptures," particularly of the prophetic books, which was made available to the Church with the Coming of Christ. The shift from one meaning to another has been accomplished unobtrusively, as the poet has given dramatic prominence to the Prophets in their prison setting and to the accompanying imagery of darkness and illumination. Indeed, it may in some sense be misleading to say that the figure of the "Key" is present in this division after the first few lines. But there can be hardly any question that the interpretations of that figure were present in the poet's mind when his material took the shape it did. One interpretation he associates explicitly, though briefly, with his description of the image. The other, the more common exegetical one, governed his development of the dramatic petition of the Prophets and the ensuing meditation on prophecy and mystery as they pertain to the Advent. Like Amalarius (CV.1268), who associated the *Clavis David* antiphon with the "spiritus intellectus," [10] the Old English poet thought of the "Key" as unlocking the meaning of Holy Writ. It may even be that his choice of the epithet *reccend* to open this section was influenced as much by other meanings of the verb *reccan,* such as "to unfold a tale," "to unravel a difficult case," or "to unfold the meaning of anything, to explain, interpret, expound," as it was by the obvious sense, "to rule, govern." In any case, it is indisputable that by the second part of the section this interpretation had risen uppermost in his imagination.

Finally, one may note the extraordinary effect that the range of meanings for the Christian figure has upon the "character" of the petitioning voice. In the first half the imprisoned speakers yearn with passionate longing in their great need. They seem to be awaiting the coming of light. But with line 70b, *þe he to wuldre forlet,* the Advent, in one sense at least, is a thing of the past. Then, in the second half of the section, they speak with great assurance of the gracious fulfillment of prophecy. The voice throughout this division may be identified as that of the Patriarchs and Prophets in limbo, but the manner of presentation is highly suggestive and relates the historic situation to the present, existential condition of the Christian, participating in the liturgical expression of the Advent. The Prophets are heard first in the generalized darkness of the Old Dispensation, then at that moment preceding release which is described in the apocryphal Gospel of Nicodemus, when John had brought the news of His coming to earth and the descent to limbo was momentarily and most anxiously expected. Finally, they are seen as the light begins to appear. But it is as yet only an internal light, which clarifies their prophetic utterances and gives them a triumphant assurance of the working of grace. It may be thought of as that overpower-

10. See Campbell, *Advent Lyrics,* p. 82.

ing Splendor, not yet fully realized, which will harrow hell. The Redemption of mankind (33 ff) is implicit from the moment of Incarnation (35b ff), and it is doubtless prophecies of Advent which are said to be fulfilled (42 ff). But the operation of redemptive grace within the individual soul, prefigured by the release of hell's captives, may be thought of as later in time. Thus the Prophets may view the Redemption as both accomplished and still to come. The emphasis, in this division, upon temporal process, upon kinds and growth of illumination, is responsible for the contact between the historical type and its metahistorical counterpart, mankind awaiting the renewal of Advent at the liturgical celebration. Both are in a state of troubled expectancy, yet both "know" that He will come and—in a sense valid even for the Prophets—that He has come.

This fluidity of the temporal perspective is, of course, characteristic of the typological imagination.[11] The human response of the petitioner reflects and varies with the shifting figure of divine activity. With the primary types as with the responding voice, the poet has made his transitions elliptically, subtly. The coherence depends more upon typological significance than upon narrative fixity or visual imagery. Time and appearance alter, now imperceptibly, now abruptly, but the timeless relation of divine activity and human response remains, continuous, changing, purposefully coherent. This section is an excellent example of the way in which typological meditation proceeds.

In spite of the muting of the motifs of divine power, the poet has introduced important figural material, which is to emerge shortly with great resonance. To the image of the "Sun" he will return in the *Oriens* section, after the prophecy of the Virgin Birth has been further explored. The transition from the preceding division was made by association of architectural figures, though again the emphasis was more on meaningful action than on picture. Now it is the most comprehensive and impressive of these images which will command his attention—the vision of the heavenly city, Jerusalem.

11. See Charity, *Events and Their Afterlife*, p. 168: Typology "is an existential address from the past or the future action of God to a present which is obscurely—but to faith really—analogous with and caught up in that action. It is the prophet's or the historian's, or the evangelist's chief way of turning prophecy, or history, or gospel to challenge."

An excellent discussion of the temporal ambiguities in the *Advent* is given by Roger Lass, "Poem as Sacrament: Transcendence of Time in the *Advent Sequence* from the Exeter Book," *Annuale Mediaevale*, 7 (1966), 3–15. Lass' view is substantially that presented here, but appeared too late for extended discussion in my text.

Division III

III. Eala sibbe gesihð,   sancta Hierusalem,   50
cynestola cyst,   Cristes burglond,
engla eþelstol,   ond þa ane in þe
saule soðfæstra   simle gerestað,
wuldrum hremge.   Næfre wommes tacn
in þam eardgearde   eawed weorþeð,   55
ac þe firena° gehwylc   feor abugeð,
wærgðo ond gewinnes.   Bist to wuldre full
halgan hyhtes,   swa þu gehaten eart.
Sioh nu sylfa þe geond   þas sidan gesceaft,
swylce rodores hrof   rume geondwlitan   60
ymb healfa gehwone,   hu þec heofones cyning
siðe geseceð,   ond sylf cymeð,
nimeð eard in þe,   swa hit ær gefyrn
witgan wisfæste   wordum sægdon,
cyðdon Cristes gebyrd,   cwædon þe to frofre,   65
burga betlicast.   Nu is þæt bearn cymen,
awæcned to wyrpe   weorcum ° Ebrea,
bringeð blisse þe,   benda onlyseð
niþum genedde.°   Nearoþearfe conn,
hu se earma sceal   are gebidan.   70

III. O vision of peace, Sancta Hierusalem,   50
Greatest of royal thrones, city of Christ,
Native seat of angels—in you they alone,
The souls of the faithful, forever rest,
Exultant in glories. Never sign of stain
Within that habitation is seen,   55
But all violence avoids you far,
All sinfulness and struggle. You are gloriously full
Of sacred hope—thus you are spoken of.
Look now around you at the wide creation;
Broadly survey the roof of the sky   60
On every side; [see] how the King of heaven
In journey seeks you and comes Himself,
Makes his home in you, as thus long before
Prophets fast in wisdom uttered in words,
Made known the birth of Christ, spoke to you with comfort,   65
Most excellent of cities. Now is the Child come,
Born to transform the work of the Hebrews;
He brings bliss to you, loosens your bonds,
Imposed by malice. He knows the anxiety
In which the impoverished must wait for grace.   70

O Hierusalem, civitas Dei summi: leva in circuitu oculos tuos, et vide Dominum tuum, quia jam veniet solvere te a vinculis.

THE *HIERUSALEM* ANTIPHON, WHICH IS THE SOURCE OF THE THIRD division, is the first of the "added O's" we encounter. It cannot be fixed with any certainty in medieval liturgical practice. The prominence of Jerusalem in the imagery of Advent is, however, attested by the fact that one Sunday of the Season was particularly consecrated to praise of the "City of God." Liturgical variations on the motif remind us how closely it is allied to the figures we have just been investigating. I have used the term "divine Power" to describe one of the major themes of the first two divisions, and a variant of the antiphon cited above substitutes the phrase "vide potentiam regis" for the second imperative. The opening verses of a hymn by Prudentius, intoned on the second Sunday of Advent, make the connection with the "Church" imagery of the *Rex gentium* section even more apparent:

Urbs beata Jerusalem, dicta pacis visio,
Quae construitur in coelis vivis ex lapidibus.[1]

The symbol of Jerusalem frequents patristic typology with a persistence equal to that with which its literal counterpart dominates the history of the Jewish people. It was perhaps inevitable that the city which was the habitation of the chosen people of God should typify the eternal home of those upon whom God's final choice had fallen. According to an established pattern of ecclesiastical thought, the Jewish reality became the Christian symbol; the praise and abuse of the Psalmist and Prophets was exchanged for the exegesis and eulogy of the Fathers. With the new heaven and new earth of the Apocalyptic vision came the new city, the "civitas sancta Jerusalem" (21:10), adorned as a bride for her bridegroom, "sponsa, uxor Agni" (21:9). It was a city without a temple, for "the Lord God al-

1. "Blessed City of Jerusalem, called the 'vision of peace' and constructed in heaven of living stones." See Guido Maria Dreves, *Analecta hymnica medii aevi, 51* (55 vols. Leipzig, 1886–1922), p. 110.

mighty is the temple thereof, and the Lamb" (21:22). Upon these and other apostolic revelations the Fathers were to found their broad and ornate structures of allegory.

But the vision of the New Jerusalem was obviously inadequate to satisfy all the symbolic opportunities of the many scriptural allusions to the City of David. The interpretation was, however, adjusted to the immediate demands of each verse, and the resultant mass of explications seems to defy categorization. John Cassian (XLIX.963–64) [2] has, however, already simplified the task, and his results are useful. Of the fourfold symbol for which the city of Jerusalem provides the literal or historical level, the allegorical intrepretation is the "temporal Church of Christ diffused throughout the whole world" (cf. Isa. 62:6); the tropological is "the soul of man which is frequently praised or blamed by God under this name" (cf. Isa. 60:1); and the anagogical is "that heavenly city of God which is mother of us all" (cf. Psalm 121:3). These levels of exegesis, in particular the allegorical and anagogical, are well substantiated in the patrology of all periods.

As early as Athanasius (*PG* [3] XXVII.283) the terrestrial Jerusalem was equated with the Church. Gregory (LXXIX.526, 506), in his *Commentary on the Canticles,* designates Jerusalem, "beautiful and loving, sweet and comely" (Canticle 6:3) as the Holy Church, "which is our mother, assiduously contemplating perpetual peace." Bede (XCIV.72), following Augustine (XXXVII.1106), contrasts Jerusalem ("Ecclesiam Christi") and Babylon ("confusionem peccatorum"), Jesus ("sacerdotem magnum") and Nebuchadnezzar ("diabolam").

Traces of the tropological, or moral, interpretation are also discovered in Gregory (LXXIX.597): "By Jerusalem, we understand that holy soul, which looks toward the future peace of the saints with the intuition of the mind"; and in the abbot Godefrid (CLXXIV.159): "In this figure the whole Church at once, or separately one blessed congregation, or as you please, any one faithful soul may be understood." [4]

However, it is obviously the mystical exposition of the Book of Revelation which triumphs over all other interpretations and indicates how they are all interrelated. For St. Hilary (IX.662) the building of the earthly city, the construction of the temple, and the institution of the tabernacle prefigure the "speciem aeternae illius et coelestis civitatis." This supernal city, according to Cassiodorus (LXX.1089), is "true peace and happiness,

---

2. See also Rabanus Maurus (CXII.966).
3. *Patrologia graeca.*
4. See also Cassiodorus (LXX.1089).

because there the saints are so joyful in their reward, that there may be
no cause for lamentation over sin." The celestial country is therefore the
"sanctae animae" by the same metonymy through which Rabanus Maurus
(CXII.966) claims that the earthly Jerusalem may also indicate the "habi-
tatores illius civitatis." It is an easy step to refer to this blessed congregation
of holy spirits as the eternal Church. Augustine (XLIII.409), in explaining
how to differentiate the figurative from the literal references to Jerusalem,
cites as a supreme example the close of the Gospel of St. Luke, where the
gathering of the Apostles in Jerusalem clearly typifies the beginnings of the
Church: "We must not understand Jerusalem as the city we can see," he
continues, "but as a figurative representation of the whole Church in a
spiritual sense—the Church which is eternal in heaven and in part a pilgrim
here on earth." Thus, as the celestial Jerusalem is mirrored in the terrestrial,
the eternal Church and congregation of saints is prefigured in the temporal
Church and its faithful believers. In the same vein Gregory (LXXVI.938)
comments on the verse, "Jerusalem, which is built as a city" (Psalm
121:3): "Because that vision of inner peace is constructed of the congregation of holy citizens, the celestial Jerusalem is built as a city. Although
in this land of pilgrimage it is beaten with whips and buffeted by tribu-
lations, its stones are daily being hewn square. And it is this very city, the
holy Church of course, which will reign in heaven, but now is afflicted on
earth." For Augustine (XXXVI.70, 122) and others who followed his
applied etymology [5] it was more convenient to see in Sion, which was
thought to mean "speculatio," a representation of the temporal Church,
"where daily, attention is directed upward to the contemplation of the
glory of God," and reserve Jerusalem for that Church "which is to be, the
city of the saints already participating in the angelic life." For Jerusalem
was interpreted "visio pacis," and the "speculation" must precede the
"vision," just as this Church upon earth precedes that which is promised,
a city immortal and eternal. And it is through speculation that one may
arrive at the vision; through a holy life of faith that one may join the
sainted congregation; through the earthly Church that one may enter its
heavenly image; through the terrestrial Jerusalem (or Sion) that one may
attain the celestial city.

It will now be obvious that the Old English poet was familiar with all of
these allegorical possibilities as well as with the etymology, "visio pacis,"
which he translates in the first half-line of this section, balancing it with the
Latin name:

5. See, for example, St Prosper (LI.380) and Rupert (CLXIX.71).

Eala sibbe gesihð,[6] sancta Hierusalem. (50)

The anagogical signification dominates the opening lines of the paraphrase, where the poet depicts the celestial City as an ideal Germanic society. Christ occupies the royal seat, and the angels and saints fill the position of retainers:

cynestola cyst,   Cristes burglond,
engla eþelstol,   ond þa ane in þe
saule soðfæstra   simle gerestað,
wuldrum hremge. (51–54a)

This is the kingdom which Christ forsook when He came to earth to redeem mankind and opened the way back to the city of life and light. This eternal resting place is the reward controlled by the Key of David, which the sacrifice of Christ has made available to fallen mankind. The anagogical allusions of these earlier divisions are now brought into sharp symbolic focus. But with the reference to the "souls of the believers," who exult in their glories like warriors with victorious booty, the poet has also touched on the allegorical level of interpretation, the "living stones" of the Church. So St. Prosper of Aquitaine (LI.372) has described it: "by virtue of the union of all the saints, one house and one temple and one city, whose structure rises from the beginning to the end, with the Lord as builder."

Properly, however, this level of meaning refers to the Church on earth, "toto orbe diffusa," and it is the terrestrial Jerusalem which dominates the remainder of the division. The identification of Jerusalem and the Church is responsible for the following lines of the text:

6. For the popularity of this etymology in Anglo-Saxon England, there is ample evidence. Cook (p. 82) cites two references in the Homilies of Ælfric (*1.*210, *2.*66) in which Jerusalem is explained as *sibbe gesihð*, and an Old English gloss of Aldhelm's *De laudibus virginitatis* which renders "[per portas] coelestis Hierosolymae" as *þære heofonlicra sibgesyhðe*. See also the *Blickling Homilies,* ed. Richard Morris (London, 1874–76), pp. 79, 81; and the Old English Version of Gregory's *Cura Pastoralis,* ed. Henry Sweet (London, 1871–72), pp. 160, 161. The appearance of the same words in *Guðlac* (813–16) is hardly accidental:

Hierusalem,
þær hi to worulde   wynnum motun
Godes onsyne   georne bihealdan,
sibbe ond gesihðe.

An emendation of 816a on the pattern of line 50a of the *Advent* would perhaps restore an original reading.

            Næfre wommes tacn
in þam eardgearde   eawed weorþeð,
ac þe firena gehwylc   feor abugeð,
wærgðo ond gewinnes.   (54b–57a)

The language of the Song of Songs was appropriated by St. Paul for his picture of the glorious Church, "having neither spot, nor wrinkle, nor any such thing, but . . . holy and immaculate" (Eph. 5:27), and these and similar epithets quickly developed, by virtue of such commentaries as Gregory's, into exegetical commonplaces for the Church and its allegorical counterpart, the city of Jerusalem. Some of these phrases provide excellent glosses for the Old English text. Augustine (XXXVII.1493), for example, speaks of the city as "libera a peccato," and much later Peter Damian (CXLIV.565) specifies an interpretation: "sine macula criminis, sine ruga simulationis." [7]

Though it is usually only the celestial City which can be imagined as an immaculate counterpart of the universal Church, the Old English poet makes it clear by the phrase *in þam eardgearde* that he is thinking of the terrestrial as well. He seems, in fact, quite willing to confound the heavenly and earthly cities, for reasons which will be shortly apparent. In the next sentence, for example, he might well be looking upward again, recollecting, as Cook has suggested (p. 82), the Psalmist's words, "Gloriosa dicta sunt de te civitas Dei" (86:3):

            Bist to wuldre full
halgan hyhtes,   swa þu gehaten eart.   (57b–58)

Since, however, *hyht* may mean "joy" but more commonly expresses "hope" or "joyous expectation," [8] the emotion denoted may refer equally to the dwellers in the earthly city or Church, whom one late commentator (Alanus de Insulis, CCX.94) has called "holy souls, who through faith and hope live in contemplation," referring to the etymology of Sion as "speculatio." In any case, once the poet takes up the imperative section of his antiphonal source, he expands in such a way as to make the terrestrial reference again explicit. "Vide Dominum tuum" becomes:

Sioh . . .
        hu þec heofones cyning
siðe geseceð,   ond sylf cymeð,
nimeð eard in þe.   (59a, 61b–63a)

   7. "free from sin" and "without spot of wrongdoing, without wrinkle of dissimulation."
   8. See lines 99, 119, and 142.

It is clear by this time that the poet is thinking of still another typological explanation for the earthly Jerusalem. Its spotlessness and its function as a receptacle for the approaching Child suggest an appropriate figure for the Blessed Virgin. Though this interpretation does not appear to have been a common one in the early Middle Ages, Cook [9] has uncovered some examples. Rabanus (CXII.897) adds it to Cassian's list as an explication of the verse of Psalm 86 cited above; St. Fulgentius (LXV.454) lists, as a divine oracle foretelling the Incarnation, the words following shortly upon it: "Shall not Mother Sion say: This man and that man were born in her? and the Highest himself has founded her?"; and a hymn of Venantius Fortunatus (LXXXVIII.277) confirms the identity of "Mater Sion" and the Virgin Mary. But an example from a much later period shows the kind of association which the Old English poet anticipated in the structuring of his typological material. In a sermon on the Annunciation, Alanus de Insulis (CCX.202) describes the entrance of Christ into a "castellum" through golden gates, which were undisturbed by His progress. This was the famous city of Jerusalem in which the great Solomon constructed his Temple. Who other than the Blessed Virgin can be intended by the Jerusalem, "vision of peace," "in which reposed the peace of eternity, in which the true Solomon, that is Christ, constructed the temple of his own body?"

Like Alanus, the poet of the *Advent* sees the figure of Jerusalem as the climax of the "Temple" imagery with which the poetic fragment began. In this section we have returned to the dominant figuration of "divine Power" of the poem's opening lines. The City in its celestial aspect is the logical outcome of the development of architectural images in the first part of the "Clavis David" section, with its *eadgan upwegas* and *wlitigan wilsiþes*. The City in its terrestrial condition is imagined in terms of a subdued allusion to the mystery of the Virgin Birth, which was explicitly described in the second part of the preceding division and will again come to the fore in the next. This short section, then, which seems an innocuous, close paraphrase of its antiphonal source, is in fact bound by an intricate pattern of thematic development to what precedes and follows. Nor is the contrapuntal motif which became so structurally prominent in the "Key" division entirely forgotten. This short Jerusalem movement draws to a close with a brief statement of the theme which rehearses the words of those Prophets who foresaw the birth of Christ (63b–66a), and, finally, it recalls poignantly the image of wretched man awaiting in fettered captivity the Advent of his Savior (68b–70).

9. In *Philologische Studien: Festgabe für Eduard Sievers* (Halle, 1896), pp. 23–25, and *Christ,* p. 81.

Division IV

IV. "Eala wifa wynn   geond wuldres þrym,
fæmne freolicast   ofer ealne foldan sceat
þæs þe æfre sundbuend   secgan hyrdon,
arece us þæt geryne   þæt þe of roderum cwom,
hu þu eacnunge   æfre onfenge   75
bearnes þurh gebyrde,   ond þone gebedscipe
æfter monwisan   mod ne cuðes.
Ne we soðlice   swylc ne gefrugnan
in ærdagum   æfre gelimpan,
þæt ðu in sundurgiefe   swylce befenge;   80
ne we þære wyrde   wenan þurfon
toweard in tide.   Huru treow in þe
weorðlicu wunade,   nu þu wuldres þrym
bosme gebære,   ond no gebrosnad wearð
mægðhad se micla.   Swa eal manna bearn   85
sorgum sawað,   swa eft ripað,
cennað to cwealme."
               Cwæð sio eadge mæg
symle sigores full,   sancta Maria:
"Hwæt is þeos wundrung   þe ge wafiað,
ond geomrende   gehþum mænað,   90
sunu Solimæ   somod his dohtor?
Fricgað þurh fyrwet   hu ic fæmnan had,
mund minne geheold,   ond eac modor gewearð
mære meotudes suna.   Forþan þæt monnum nis
cuð geryne,   ac Crist onwrah   95
in Dauides   dyrre mægan
þæt is Euan scyld   eal forpynded,
wærgða aworpen,   ond gewuldrad is
se heanra had.   Hyht is onfangen
þæt nu bletsung mot   bæm gemæne,   100
werum ond wifum,   a to worulde forð
in þam uplican   engla dreame
mid soðfæder   symle wunian."

IV. "O joy of womankind in the majesty of heaven,
Noblest woman over all the earth's regions
Of whom sea-dwellers have ever heard spoken,
Expound that mystery which came to you from the sky—
How you ever conceived a child,   75
Became pregnant, and yet intercourse
According to man's ways knew not at all.
We truly have not heard of such an event
Ever occurring in former days,
As you in special grace have thus experienced;   80
Nor have we reason to expect such a fate
Any time in the future.   Indeed there has dwelt in you
A worthy trust, since you have carried in your womb
The Majesty of heaven, and your incomparable purity
Was never corrupted.   As all children of men   85
Sow in sorrow, so shall they reap;
They bring forth to death."
                      The blessed maiden spoke,
Ever full of victory, Sancta Maria:
"What is this spectacle that you wonder at
And lamenting moan with grief,   90
Sons of Salem and her daughters together?
Out of curiosity you ask how I retained my virginity
And my virtue, and yet became mother
Renowned of the Son of God.   To mankind, however,
Knowledge of this mystery is not given,   95
But Christ has revealed in David's dear kinswoman
That the guilt of Eve is all absolved,
The curse cast off, and glorified
Is the lowlier sex. Hope is entertained
That blessing now upon both together,   100
Men and women alike, henceforth forever
In the celestial consort of angels
With the true Father may eternally rest."

O Virgo virginum, quomodo fiet istud, quia nec primam similem visa es nec habere sequentem? Filiae Hierusalem, quid me admiramini? Divinum est mysterium hoc quod cernitis.

THIS, THE MOST VENERABLE OF THE "ADDITIONAL" ANTIPHONS, IS listed in the Gregorian *Liber* as the eighth of the "Antiphonae majores." Amalarius (CV.1269) found no difficulty in relating the addition to his numerical symbolism, based on the seven Gifts of the Holy Spirit: "This antiphon reveals that Man, Who received carnal form from Mary, and Who alone is perfect among the rest of mankind, because the sevenfold Spirit dwells in Him alone." As his authority he cites Augustine: "Seven is the number which perfects, while the eighth clarifies and demonstrates that which is perfect." In this section of the *Advent* poem there seems also to be a sense of clarification and demonstration. This is to a great extent a reflection of the character of the antiphon, but that this passage has the effect of bringing a larger "movement" of the poem to its inevitable conclusion is equally a testimony to the way in which the poet had ordered his material in the preceding divisions.

At this point the poem seems to undergo a distinct alteration in tone. We have begun in the realm of large, abstract figures, the "lapis angularis," the "clavis David," and the "civitas Dei," interspersed with passages of lament and supplication. In the second division the antiphonal exclamation gradually emerged as part of the petition of the "dwellers in darkness," who were only obliquely identified. With this fourth section the poem erupts vividly into direct address and dramatic dialogue. The citizens of Jerusalem—those who have, a few lines back, been figuratively exhorted to prepare for the Child's Coming—are now in the presence of the astonishing reality. They question Mary directly about her extraordinary pregnancy:

Arece us þæt geryne   þæt þe of roderum cwom,
hu þu eacnunge   æfre onfenge
bearnes þurh gebyrde,   ond þone gebedscipe
æfter monwisan   mod ne cuðes.   (74–77)

The language here quite explicitly recalls the similar discussion of the mystery in the *Clavis David* section:

þæt wæs geworden   butan weres frigum,
þæt þurh bearnes gebyrd   bryd eacen wearð.
Nænig efenlic þam,   ær ne siþþan,
in worlde gewearð   wifes geacnung.   (37–40)

The recurrence is not purely a linguistic matter; the hypothetical speakers are also to be identified. In the *Advent* the spokesman for all mankind, awaiting the Coming of the Lord, takes many forms. The voice is at times personal and contemporary (or, one might say, metahistorical), looking for a spiritual advent and relying for inspiration upon the liturgical Season. At other times the speaker is placed in a quasi-historical context, where the "real" Advent is as yet only expectation. The Patriarchs and Prophets who dwell in darkness are granted a privileged condition for having recognized the Coming, either through typological activity or through prophetic utterance. The citizens of Jerusalem, here introduced as allegorical personae, are to be associated with them. The poet extends the antiphonal text, making them of both sexes, *sunu Solimæ somod his dohtor* (91), and they are also darkly in the presence of the mysterious event. In this poem, then, as in *The Waste Land,*[1] all of the participants of each sex melt together and unite in a single voice, though here the conflation of the dramatis personae is made possible by typological tradition rather than poetical fiat.

The daughters of Jerusalem (or Sion), who figure as a chorus to the Song of Songs, were easily caught up in the ecclesiastical allegorization of that poem and were interpreted as "sanctae animae" or as "Ecclesia" itself. These alternatives are offered by Rabanus Maurus (CXI.379) in his *De Universo* and are supported by such scriptural passages as Zephaniah 3:14, Psalm 149:2 and Joel 2:1. In Gregory's exposition of the Canticum (LXXIX.530) these women are referred to as "daughters of the Church, who, contemplating eternal life while in this flesh, are raised from the pilgrim Church [on earth] to that which reigns [in heaven]." Later exegesis, perhaps anticipated by the Old English poet in his emphasis on the "weaker

1. See Eliot's famous note to line 218 of that poem: "Tiresias, although a mere spectator and not indeed a 'character,' is yet the most important personage in the poem, uniting all the rest. Just as the one-eyed merchant, seller of currants, melts into the Phoenician Sailor, and the latter is not wholly distinct from Ferdinand Prince of Naples, so all the women are one woman, and the two sexes meet in Tiresias. What Tiresias *sees*, in fact, is the substance of the poem."

sex" (97–101), treats the "filiae" as "weak souls, though devout." Such
terms are to be found in the writings of the abbot Wolbero (CXCV.1205)
and Adam the Scot (CXCVIII.322), the latter of whom explains: "weakness is denoted by their feminine sex, and devotion, by the place of peace."
But in general, the allegorization of the "citizens" follows that of the City
and refers either to the Church or to its congregation of saintly souls. One
variation, however, provides interesting evidence for the typological conflation discussed above. The abbot Rupert (CLXVIII.481), in a discussion of Hebrews 12:22–23, identifies the "inhabitants of Jerusalem" as the
"early Church of the Patriarchs, Prophets, and other saints, which was
bound together in grief while it was awaiting Christ, having as it were
neither king nor counsellor, since it held Him only in promise and hope."
So, too, the "sons and daughters of Jerusalem" of our poem speak for all
those in expectation of the Coming, and specifically for those who under
the Old Dispensation saw only through a glass darkly.

The wonder and bewilderment of these "citizens" is represented in a
more or less naturalistic fashion, but the Old Testament mentality is perhaps apparent in the proverbial folk-wisdom, with its gloomy sense of
justice:

> Swa eal manna bearn
> sorgum sawað, swa eft ripað,
> cennað to cwealme. (85b–87a)

The allusion, in spite of the echo of Galatians 6:7–8, is primarily to the
curse upon Eve of pain in childbearing (Gen. 3:16). This challenge to
her sex gives Mary an opportunity to assert her typological relation to Eve:

> þæt is Euan scyld eal forpynded,
> wærgða aworpen, ond gewuldrad is
> se heanra had. (97–99a)

This most venerable of Marian types is found among the Greek Fathers
only a generation or two after the Apostolic Era, and the "second Eve"
became the commonest of epithets for the Blessed Virgin. More than just
an ingenious parody of Paul's phrase for Christ, the "second Adam," it developed into an integral part of the Marian doctrine, an idea of "the highest and most important signification." [2] Two passages ascribed to the great
Latin Doctors will suffice to give some sense of the ingenuity with which
the type was expanded and woven into Christian doctrine. In a pseudo-

2. Livius, *The Blessed Virgin,* p. 41.

Ambrosian sermon (XVII.692) the motif is developed with terse and effective rhetoric:

> As evil came about through a woman, so, too, through a woman came
> goodness: because through Eve we fell, through Mary we stand: . . .
> Eve caused us to be damned through the fruit of a tree, Mary absolves
> us through the gift of a tree, for Christ hung from a tree like a fruit . . .
> Through Eve we were born, through Mary we rule; through Eve we
> were brought down to earth, through Mary raised to heaven: . . . In
> Eve, then, Mary was present; through Mary Eve was revealed.

A sermon, once attributed to Augustine (XXXIX.1991), develops a point which is perhaps more immediately pertinent to the Old English text at hand:

> The restoration of woman was brought about by Mary, because through
> her women are shown to have been exempted from the harm of the orig-
> inal judgment. The three curses on Eve are seen to have been removed
> by the three blessings on Mary. For it was said to Eve: "In pain and
> sorrow thou shalt conceive; yet thy desire shall be for thy husband, and
> he shall have dominion over thee" (Genesis 3:16). Women, therefore,
> are subject to three evils which do not attend on Mary: pain, sorrow,
> and servitude. Listen, on the contrary, to those three most glorious
> blessings by which Mary is raised on high: the angelic salutation, di-
> vine benediction, and the fullness of grace.[3]

In the speech of the "sancta Maria" of our poem the typological relation to Eve is the focal point of her reply. She dismisses the curiosity of
the "citizens" in words that recall the *Clavis David* once again: *Forþan
þæt monnum nis cuð geryne* (94b–95a) is the corollary of *þæt degol wæs,
dryhtnes geryne* (41). But though much remains mysterious, the undoing
of Eve's curse by the kinsman of David may be spoken of. What Christ
has revealed through the Incarnation is a supreme manifestation of divine
Power, in which the woman's role and the unnatural occasion are over-
shadowed by the anagogical significance. Human understanding of the divine mysteries is both impossible and irrelevant. What should matter to
these "sons and daughters of Jerusalem," the Virgin seems to imply, is not
the satisfaction of their curiosity but their redemption from the curse on
their forefathers and the promise of eternal life:

3. For further reference, see ibid., pp. 35–59, 69–74.

> Hyht is onfangen
> þæt nu bletsung mot   bæm gemæne,[4]
> werum ond wifum,   a to worulde forð
> in þam uplican   engla dreame
> mid soðfæder   symle wunian.   (99b–103)

Thus the conclusion of the *Virgo virginum* section returns us to the vision of the celestial Jerusalem, which was elaborated in the preceding division and anticipated in the second. Indeed, the *Hierusalem* passage might well be considered the "setting" of this exchange between the Virgin and its "citizens." The allegorical discussion of the terrestrial city, with its implied relevance to the Incarnation and Virgin Birth, leads smoothly into the dialogue where what had existed in typological obscurity is now the explicit subject of discourse. And just as the "scene" is drawn from the *Hierusalem* passage, the personae are descended from the petitioners of the *Clavis David* section. Their concern with the mystery of the virginal pregnancy has become the focus of a quickened verbal exchange, in which one of the poet's favorite themes is restated with an emergent historical realization and a new dramatic tonality.

4. A similar sentiment is found in the Nativity sermons of St. Augustine (XXXVIII.996): "Exsultent viri, exsultent feminae: Christus vir est natus, ex femina est natus; et uterque sexus est honoratus."

Division V

V. Eala earendel,   engla beorhtast
ofer middangeard   monnum sended,   105
ond soðfæsta   sunnan leoma,
torht ofer tunglas,   þu tida gehwane
of sylfum þe   symle inlihtes.
Swa þu, god of gode   gearo° acenned,
sunu soþan fæder,   swegles in wuldre   110
butan anginne   æfre wære,
swa þec nu for þearfum   þin agen geweorc
bideð þurh byldo,   þæt þu þa beorhtan us
sunnan onsende,   ond þe sylf cyme
þæt ðu inleohte   þa þe longe ær,   115
þrosme beþeahte   ond in þeostrum her,
sæton sinneahtes;   synnum bifealdne
deorc deaþes sceadu   dreogan sceoldan.
Nu we hyhtfulle   hælo gelyfað
þurh þæt word godes   weorodum brungen,   120
þe on frymðe wæs   fæder ælmihtigum
efenece mid god,   ond nu eft gewearð
flæsc firena leas   þæt seo fæmne gebær
geomrum to geoce.   God wæs mid us
gesewen butan synnum;   somod eardedon   125
mihtig meotudes bearn   ond se monnes sunu
geþwære on þeode.   We þæs þonc magon
secgan sigedryhtne   symle bi gewyrhtum,
þæs þe he hine sylfne us   sendan wolde.

V. O rising Light, brightest of angels
Over the earth sent to mankind, 105
And righteous ray of the sun,
Resplendent beyond stars, all seasons
With your presence You endlessly illumine.
As You, God of God truly begotten,
Son of the true Father, in the glory of the heavens 110
Have ever been without beginning,
So now in distress Your own creation
Implores most boldly that You send to us
The bright sun, and come Yourself
That You may illumine those who long since, 115
Covered with smoke and darkness here,
Have sat in eternal night; enfolded by sin,
They had to endure the dark shadow of death.
Now with hope we believe in salvation
Brought to the multitudes through the Word of God 120
Which was in the beginning with the almighty Father,
Coeternal with God, and now without violence
Has become flesh which the woman bore
As a comfort to the mournful. God was among us
Seen without sin; together have lived 125
The mighty Child of the Lord and the Son of man,
In harmony on earth. For this we may give thanks,
Endlessly, fittingly, to the Lord of victories
That He would send to us His very self.

O Oriens, splendor lucis aeternae, et sol justitiae: veni, et illumina seden-
tes in tenebris et umbra mortis.

ITH THIS SECTION WE RETURN TO THE "GREAT O'S" OF *ADVENT* and their magnificent typological invocations. In the Old English text there is the impression of a new "movement" beginning, a new "attack" on one of the major themes. Not that the imagery is new to the poem. The figure of the sun and its illumination has already been seriously introduced in the *Clavis David* section, in response to the phrase of the petition which that antiphon has in common with the *Oriens:* "sedentes in tenebris et umbra mortis." Here, once again, the contrapuntal motif of the "dwellers in darkness" is translated with great poetic density:

> . . . Cyme
> þæt ðu inleohte   þa þe longe ær,
> þrosme beþeahte   ond in þeostrum her,
> sæton sinneahtes;   synnum bifealdne
> deorc deaþes sceadu   dreogan sceoldan.   (114–18)

The difference in the character of this division comes not from the familiar figures but from the introduction of a new mode of thematic presentation. The *Advent* began with impressive typological images, then turned and will soon return to a somewhat realistic contemplation of the historical event. Now the poet interjects unexpectedly an unadorned and abstract statement of doctrine. But this new "mode," like the figurative and dramatic ones, is a response to the typological associations of the antiphonal phrases.

The Latin participial noun "oriens" can mean either "that which rises" —i.e. a heavenly body, the sun—or "the quarter from which the sun rises" —i.e. the east. In the latter sense the "Orient" figured in several prophetic utterances which were to lend substance to later Messianic and Christian symbolism: "Behold the glory of the God of Israel came in by way of the east" (Ezech. 43:2), and, with a possible clue to the sequence in the

Old English poem, "Look about you, o Jerusalem, toward the east, and see
the joy which comes to you from God" (Baruch 4:36, also 5:5). The
Liber formularum spiritalis intelligentiae of St. Eucherius (L.741), in a
catalogue *de supernis creaturis,* identifies "oriens" with "Salvator," "because the light originates in that quarter."

The primary New Testament source for the "oriens" figure is the words
of Zacharias, father of the Baptist: "The Orient from on high has visited
us" (Luke 1:78), which Rabanus Maurus (CXII.1012) translates, "Christ
came to us from heaven." This text was repeatedly associated with a striking verse in Zechariah, which the Vulgate misleadingly [1] translates: "Behold a man, the Orient is his name" (6:12). Jerome in his commentary on
Zechariah (XXV.1439) harmonizes these two texts and adds the "sol
justitiae" image from Malachi (4:2). The latter figure was, of course, related to the Day of Judgment, "which will be light to the holy, darkness to
sinners" (XXV.1575). Though this aspect of the solar typology is not
touched on in the *Oriens* section, it may well have influenced our poet's
treatment of the "Key of David" motif and encouraged the introduction of
"light" imagery at that point.

It was perhaps the third element of the antiphonal invocation which
prompted the theological turn given to this section. The "splendor lucis
aeternae" is an adaptation of a phrase in the Prologue to the Epistle to the
Hebrews, which is worth citing as a whole:

1. The Hebrew word in Zechariah 3:8 and 6:12, which Jerome reads as
"oriens," was "tsemach," meaning "sprout," "shoot," or "branch," and was
taken by the Prophet primarily from Jeremiah 23:5 and 33:15, where the
Messiah is promised as a "righteous sprout" raised up unto David. This expression was associated by Jerome (XXV.1439) with the Tree of Jesse, father
of David, whose family had fallen into humiliation, but was exalted by the
Messiah in justice and glory. See C. F. Keil and F. Delitzsch, *Biblical Commentary on the Old Testament, 25* (25 vols. Edinburgh, 1857–78), 259–60,
299; and C. A. Briggs, S. R. Driver, and A. Plummer, *The International
Critical Commentary, 24* (35 vols. New York, 1895–1920), 186–87, and
3, 43, on Luke 1:78. Jerome (XXV.1456) himself understood the Hebrew
word perfectly. He writes it "sema" and glosses it as "germen," interpreting
Zechariah 6:12: "quia ex se repente succrescet, et ex radice sua in simili-
tudinem germinis pullulabit, qui vir aedificabit templum Domini." The earlier
association of "oriens" with Christ as a figure of "light" (in such texts as
Luke 1:78, Malachi 4:2, and Numbers 24:17) seems to suggest that Jerome
was willing, for typological purposes, to ignore the verbal distinction between
"oriens" as "sprout" and "oriens" as "rising sun."

God, Who in former days spoke to our forefathers by the prophets at sundry times and in diverse manners, in this final age has spoken to us in the Son, Whom He has made heir to the whole universe, and by Whom also He made the world. The Son, being the brightness of His glory [*splendor gloriae*] and the figure of His substance, upholding all things by the word of His power, bringing about the purgation of sins, sits on the right hand of the Majesty in heaven. (1:1–3)

The beginning of this passage, with its contrast of prophetic utterance and the activities of the Son, both manifestations of the Father, is perhaps a clue to the poet's development of these major contrapuntal configurations. But the phrase "splendor gloriae" is our immediate concern. The dogmatic substance of this text was expounded at length in a homily of St. John Chrysostom (*PG* LXIII.19 ff.), which was incorporated by Alcuin (C. 1033) in his exposition of Hebrews. Of the verse in question he writes:

> He rightly called Him "splendor gloriae," since he knew His own saying: "I am the light of the world" (John 8:12), which makes known that He is light of light, just as He is God of God, illuminating our souls and ingratiating us with His Father. By "splendor" he has in fact declared the unity of essence with God the Father, and "in a marvelous way he speaks of one substance in order to reveal two persons alike in glory and splendor."

The *Glossa ordinaria* (CXIV.643) confirms that the phrase became fixed in association with Trinitarian doctrine during the first millennium: "Here he praises Christ in terms of His divine nature, showing Him coeternal and coequal with the Father, of the same substance with Him, but different in person."

In the *Advent* paraphrase the equivalent of "splendor gloriae" does not occur among the splendid vocatives of the opening. If it is to be sought, it is rather in the words, *swegles in wuldre* (110b), which are part of the first theological statement (109–11). In the expected place at the opening we find rather *engla beorhtast* (104b), a figure which is related, however, to the same complex of ideas. The most prominent of scriptural testimonies to the use of "angelus" as an epithet for Christ is, according to St. Eucherius (L.739), the phrase from Isaiah (9:6) in the Old Latin Bible based on the Septuagint text: "magni concilii angelus." The type was explained by Augustine (XXXVIII.691) to mean "messenger of the Will of the Father," referring to the office of Christ and not His nature (XXXVIII.64), for though as a messenger He announced to mankind the kingdom of heaven,

He was in fact "Dominus omnium angelorum" and also their Creator, since "all things were made by Him" (John 1:3). When this figure is brought in conjunction with the various angels of the Apocalypse, we find ourselves returning to the imagery of the sun and light. Alcuin (C. 1129) saw the first angel, "ascending from the rising of the sun" (7:2), as Christ resurrected, announcing the joy of the new life like a new sun. He springs forth and rising, fills the entire world, illuminating the evangelical doctrines. And the abbot Rupert (CLXIX.959) brings the figuration back to the *Oriens* antiphon: "He ascended from the sunrise, to bring light to those who were sitting in darkness and in the shadow of death, ascending from those below, rising from the dead—a resurrection which to us is truly the rising of the sun." Thus, in the typological perambulations of the Fathers, we find all the figures of the antiphon and poem, "sol," "oriens" (*earendel* [2]), "splendor gloriae," and "angelus," woven tightly together, and with them the theological concern, emanating from the Prologue to Hebrews,[3] for the begetting of the Son and His coeternity with the Father.

I cannot account for Campbell's displeasure (see pp. 19–20) with the structure of this division of the poem, unless the source lie in a distaste for the theological material itself. The poet, as I see it, has worked together his doctrinal matter and his imagery into a texture of great imaginative intricacy. In so doing, he alludes to a concept which Augustine tackled again and again in his sermons on the Nativity, the "twofold generation of Christ": "Generation by the Father without a mother, and by the mother without a father: both miraculous. The first was an eternal generation, the second temporal" (XXXVIII.1006). In the Old English text, after the invocation has established the "light" figure, a complex sentence (109–18) sets up a similar series of parallels (*swa . . . , swa . . .*), by which the abstract theological statement of events which exist outside of time is related to the concrete imagery of a historical reality. The Begetting of the Son, "Deus de Deo," is set against Creation (*þin agen geweorc,* 112b); the glory of the heavens (110b) against the bright light of the sun, which will illumine earthly darkness and death; and the eternality of the Deity (*butan anginne æfre wære,* 111) against the specific moment in time when His expected Coming will put an end to the long suffering of the sinful.

2. On the equivalence of these terms, see J. E. Cross, "The 'Coeternal Beam' in the O. E. Advent Poem (Christ I) 11. 104–129," *Neophilologus, 48* (1964), 72–81.

3. Where, it might be noted, the passage cited above is followed by a discussion of the role of the angels in the scheme of salvation.

This process of relating two temporal orders is repeated in the later part of this section. It begins with a line which suggests that the poet was consciously echoing the Creed: *Nu we hyhtfulle hælo gelyfað* (119). In contrast to this *nu* is again the eternity of God (121–22a), and the timeless Word of God becomes the flesh of the present, immaculate Incarnation. As God and man are thus brought together, the syntax becomes accordingly uninvolved and the sentences become simple:

God wæs mid us
gesewen butan synnum;   somod eardedon
mihtig meotudes bearn   ond se monnes sunu
geþwære on þeode.   (124b–27a)

The mysterious union is subtly reinforced by the unexpected exchange of *bearn* and *sunu* in 126, and the theological implications of the event are suggested by the emphasis upon the sinlessness of the divine Man Who has come among the *synnum bifealdne* (117b). After this impressively controlled display of theologically resonant rhetoric, the awed simplicity of the final sentence seems most appropriate:

We þæs þonc magon
secgan sigedryhtne   symle bi gewyrhtum,
þæs þe he hine sylfne us   sendan wolde.[4]   (127b–29)

4. Cross, in "The 'Coeternal Beam'," supports, with further patristic commentary, my interpretation (arrived at independently) of the typological accord between the figural and doctrinal material of this section. His conclusions on the reflection of Trinitarian dogma in the Old English text are worth quoting in full: "This dogma of coeternity of Father and Son necessitates a belief that the Son in his Godhead took part in his own generation, and this the OE. poet infers in the last line of his sequence: 'For He willed to send Himself to us' (1. 129). The inseparability of this work is indicated again when the human petitioners refer to themselves as the Son's 'own work' (1. 112), and this belief helps to elucidate a paradox in the metaphorical part of the section where Christ who has been called 'true light of the sun' is invoked to send 'the bright sun' and come himself (1. 114). As suggested above, sunlight and sun are two names for Christ arising respectively from the interpretation or acceptance of differing Scriptural texts, so that the request for Christ to send himself and come himself is an effective way of reiterating the inseparability of Father and Son. The final paradox is presented in the phrase: 'together they lived, mighty Son of God and Son of Man' (11. 125–26), which is a dramatic way of describing Christ's retention of the Godhead in his human form. As a commonplace tag of the Fathers presents it: '. . . manens quod erat, suscipiens quod non erat'" (pp. 77–78).

Division VI

VI. Eala gæsta god,   hu þu gleawlice   130
mid noman ryhte   nemned wære
Emmanuhel,   swa hit engel gecwæð
ærest on Ebresc!   Þæt is eft gereht,
rume bi gerynum: "Nu is rodera weard,
god sylfa mid us."   Swa þæt gomele gefyrn   135
ealra cyninga cyning   ond þone clænan eac
sacerd soðlice   sægdon toweard,
swa se mæra iu,   Melchisedech,
gleaw in gæste,   godþrym onwrah
eces alwaldan.   Se wæs æ bringend,   140
lara lædend,   þam longe his
hyhtan hidercyme,   swa him gehaten wæs,
þætte sunu meotudes   sylfa wolde
gefælsian   foldan mægðe,
swylce grundas eac   gæstes mægne   145
siþe gesecan.   Nu hie softe þæs
bidon in bendum   hwonne bearn godes
cwome to cearigum.   Forþon cwædon swa,
suslum geslæhte: "Nu þu sylfa cum,
heofones heahcyning.   Bring us hælolif,   150
werigum witeþeowum,   wope forcymenum
bitrum brynetearum.   Is seo bot gelong
eal æt þe anum.   [Þu for] oferþearfum
hæftas hygegeomre   hider [gesec]es; ⁰
ne læt þe behindan,   þonne þu heonan cyrre,   155
mænigo þus micle,   ac þu miltse on us
gecyð cynelice,   Crist nergende,
wuldres æþeling,   ne læt awyrgde ofer us
onwald agan.   Læf us ecne gefean
wuldres þines,   þæt þec weorðien,   160
weoroda wuldorcyning,   þa þu geworhtes ær
hondum þinum.   Þu in heannissum
wunast wideferh   mid waldend fæder."

VI. O God of spirits, how wisely You   130
By rightful name were called
Emmanuel, as the angel spoke it
First in Hebrew, which thereafter is interpreted,
From its hidden sense plainly: "Now is God Himself,
The Guardian of the heavens, among us."   135
As sages of former times accurately foretold
The King of all kings and immaculate Priest,
So, too, of old the great Melchisedech,
Wise in spirit, revealed the divine majesty
Of the eternal Ruler. He was the bringer of laws,   140
The guide of learning, to those who long
Hoped for His coming, as it was promised them
That the Son of the Lord Himself would cleanse
The peoples of the earth, and would, moreover, in His journey,
Through the might of the Spirit, seek out the depths.   145
Patiently now, with this knowledge,
They waited in chains till the Child of God
Should come to the care-laden. Therefore they spoke thus,
Weakened by torments: "Come now Yourself,
High King of heaven. Bring us salvation,   150
Weary slaves of torture, overcome by weeping,
By bitter tears of burning. Release is dependent
All on You alone. For [their] great need
You seek here these mournful captives;
Do not leave behind You, when You turn away,   155
This great multitude, but mercy upon us
Make known royally, Christ savior,
Nobleman of glory; nor let the accursed
Hold power over us. Leave us the eternal gladness
Of Your glory, that they may worship You,   160
Glorious King of hosts, whom formerly You made
With Your own hands. You in the highest
Reside forever with the sovereign Father."

*O Emmanuel, Rex et Legifer noster, exspectatio gentium et salvator
earum: veni ad salvandum nos, Dominus Deus noster.*

THE *EMMANUEL* ANTIPHON IS WITHOUT DOUBT THE STARKEST OF
the "Great O's," quite devoid of the suggestion of concrete imagery. But the Old English poet has done admirable things with it,
while following the order of the antiphonal catalogue most scrupulously. He
has developed the invocation on the suggestion of the prophetic character of
its first element; and the petition is expanded into a dramatic utterance from
the mouths of the very Prophets he has been citing. In terms of the modes
of presentation this section provides an unobtrusive transition from the
lofty theology and awesome figures of the *Oriens* division to the unusually
realistic drama of the "Passus" which follows.

The etymology of the name "Emmanuel" further reinforces the sequence
of divisions here. The preceding unit closed, we remember, with an emphasis on the Incarnation: *God wæs mid us gesewen butan synnum* (124b–
25a). Now the phrase is repeated, this time as the interpretation of the
Hebrew name: *Nu is rodera Weard, God sylfa mid us* (134b–35a). The
etymology is found, as the Old English poet reminds us, not in the Old
Testament but in the Gospel of Matthew (1:23): "Emmanuel, quod est
interpretatum Nobiscum Deus," and is spoken by the angel of the Lord.
It was he, incidentally, who resolved those doubts of Joseph which are the
concern of the next division of our poem. The meaning of this interpretation is the reconciliation of God and man through the incarnate Christ,
which the syntax and rhetoric of the *Oriens* passage has skillfully explored,
and which the Fathers of the Church, from Tertullian (II.337) down,
consistently affirm. The testimony of Augustine (XXXIV.385) may be
taken as typical: "Emmanuel, God-with-us, has reconciled us to God, a
Man and Mediator of God and men (1 Tim. 2:5), the Word with God,
flesh among us (John 1:1,14), Word and flesh between God and us."

But the subject of the opening of the *Emmanuel* paraphrase is as much
the reconciliation of the two Testaments as it is the union of God and
man. Though the interpreting angel belongs to the New Testament, the

words cited derive from the most famous of Old Testament prophecies, that of Isaiah 7:14: "Behold a virgin shall conceive, and bear a son, and his name shall be called Emmanuel." The poet seems to know that the next words of the antiphon are also from Isaiah: "The Lord is our judge, the Lord is our lawgiver, the Lord is our king: He will save us" (33:22). These titles are also part of the testimony of the Prophets in the Old English text:

> Swa þæt gomele gefyrn
> ealra cyninga cyning   ond þone clænan eac
> sacerd soðlice   sægdon toweard. (135b–37)

The substitution of *sacerd* for the "legifer" of the antiphon enables the poet to include Melchisedech, "rex Salem, sacerdos Dei summi" (Heb. 7:1). The process by which Melchisedech *godþrym onwrah* (139b) has been thoroughly explored in the introduction to this study.[1] We may recall in this context, however, the typological elaborations of Ambrose (XVI.404) on his mysterious origins: "without a mother according to His divine nature, because He was begotten of God the Father, and of one substance with the Father; wtihout a father according to His incarnation, Who was born of a virgin; having neither beginning nor end, because He Himself is beginning and end of all, the first and the last." Melchisedech's figural significance was found not only in the mystery of his origin but also in his claim to the priesthood, his receipt of tithes, his gift of the sacramental bread and wine, and his union of circumcised and uncircumcised in one Church. Thus, as a supreme type of Christ, he ranks with Isaiah and the Prophets, and qualifies among those who wait for the Advent, *swa him gehaten wæs* (142b).[2]

The *Advent* poet now remedies the omission of "legifer" from its expected position in the paraphrase, with the epithets *æ bringend, lara lædend* (140b–41a). These terms for Christ apply equally well to Melchisedech by virtue of his superiority to the Levitical priesthood and the law of Moses. The paraphrase of the next words of the antiphon, "exspectatio gentium, et salvator earum," begins the transition from the prophetic to the dramatic passage of the division. The Old Testament figures have all been promised:

> þætte sunu meotudes   sylfa wolde
> gefælsian   foldan mægðe.   (143–44)

1. See above, pp. 10–13.
2. On the association of Prophets and prophetic types, see Auerbach, *Typologische Motive*, p. 18.

Now they are seen as waiting in expectation, full of the knowledge of prophecy and typological anticipation, but none the less fettered and prostrate with torments.

The antiphonal petition is put into a historical context and expanded with great ingenuity and feeling. Once again, as in the *Clavis David* section, the cry for mercy and salvation comes from the depths of darkness and suffering. The speech is of great beauty, and one can do no better than transcribe Campbell's enthusiastic appreciation:

> The terms *hæftas, witeþeow,* and *brynetear,* as well as the concepts of chains, tortures, and weariness, all of which had long since assumed a very conventional air, achieved a new force and a more convincing meaning when applied to the souls of the patriarchs awaiting Christ. Perhaps it is because the other poems reflect on this one, and this petition sounds like many of the others, but we are conscious throughout this portion of the poem that the *we* theme is being expanded. The souls in hell and the suffering community of living sinners become one, and there is a great intensification of the meaning and emotion of the poem. (p. 21)

One need only add, perhaps, that in the final lines of the petition the speakers remind us of much else that has gone before. They associate their Creation (161b–62a) with their dependence and their desire for salvation, that *ecne gefean wuldres þines* (159b–60a), the joy of the celestial Jerusalem. And they conclude with a simple and solemn declaration of the supremity of the Son with the Father:

> þu in heannissum
> wunast wideferh   mid waldend fæder.   (162b–63)

In this splendid division, then, the poet has shown that he could follow the order of his antiphonal source, yet give it a rationale all its own. At the same time, he garners many of the themes and motifs which have gone before and moves his poem forward to a pitch of dramatic intensity, preparing us for the passionate and realistic encounter which lies ahead.

Division VII

VII. [Mary:] "Eala Ioseph min,   Iacobes bearn,
mæg Dauides   mæran cyninges,   165
nu þu freode scealt   fæste gedælan,
alætan lufan mine,   ic lungre eam
deope gedrefed,   dome bereafod.
Forðon ic worn for þe   worde° hæbbe
sidra sorga   ond sarcwida   170
hearmes gehyred,   ond me hosp sprecað,
tornworda fela.   Ic tearas sceal
geotan geomormod.   God eaþe mæg
gehælan hygesorge   heortan minre,
afrefran feasceafte."
[Joseph:]   "Eala fæmne geong,   175
mægð Maria,   hwæt bemurnest ðu,
cleopast cearigende?   Ne ic culpan in þe,
incan ænigne,   æfre onfunde,
womma geworhtra;   ond þu þa word spricest
swa þu sylfa sie   synna gehwylcre   180
firena gefylled.   Ic to fela hæbbe
þæs byrdscypes   bealwa onfongen.
Hu mæg ic ladigan   laþan spræce,
oþþe ondsware   ænige findan
wraþum towiþere?   Is þæt wide cuð   185
þæt ic of þam torhtan   temple dryhtnes
onfeng freolice   fæmnan clæne,
womma lease,   ond nu gehwyrfed is
þurh nathwylces.°   Me nawþer deag,
secge ne swige.   Gif ic soð sprece,   190
þonne sceal Dauides   dohtor sweltan,
stanum astyrfed.   Gen strengre is
þæt ic morþor hele: scyle manswara
laþ leoda gehwam   lifgan siþþan
fracoð in folcum."

VII. [Mary:] "O my Joseph, son of Jacob,
Kinsman of David the great king,   165
Since you must now wholly renounce our vows,
Cast off my love, I am all at once
Deeply grieved, bereft of reputation.
Indeed I have heard much on your account
In words of great pity and sore reproach   170
And injury; to me they speak abuse
And many insulting words. I cannot keep from weeping,
Saddened in spirit. God may easily
Heal the sorrow of my heart,
Give comfort to the disconsolate."
[Joseph:]   "O tender child,   175
Mary virgin, why do you mourn
And cry out with such feeling? No fault in you
Nor any cause for suspicion have I found
Of wrongs committed; yet you speak
As if you yourself were filled of every sin   180
And defilement. I have had too much
Of unhappiness from this pregnancy.
How may I confute the hostile speech
Or find any answer against my enemies?
It is widely known that I,   185
From the bright temple of the Lord,
Freely received a pure woman
Without stain, and now this is all changed,
How I don't know. It does me no good
Either to speak or keep silent. If I speak the truth,   190
Then the daughter of David must die,
Crushed by stones. Still harder it is
If I conceal the crime: then should the perjurer,
Loathsome in every nation, live thereafter
Infamous to all men."

     Þa seo fæmne onwrah   195
ryhtgeryno, ond þus reordade:
"Soð ic secge þurh sunu meotudes,
gæsta geocend, þæt ic gen ne conn
þurh gemæcscipe monnes ower,
ænges on eorðan, ac me eaden wearð,   200
geongre in geardum, þæt me Gabrihel,
heofones heagengel, hælo gebodade.
Sægde soðlice þæt me swegles gæst
leoman onlyhte, sceolde ic lifes þrym
geberan, beorhtne sunu, bearn eacen godes,   205
torhtes tirfruma*n*. Nu ic his tempel eam
gefremed butan facne; in me frofre gæst
geeardode. Nu þu ealle forlæt
sare sorgceare.° Saga ecne þonc
mærum meotodes sunu þæt ic his modor gewearð, 210
fæmne forð seþeah, ond þu fæder cweden
woruldcund bi wene. Sceolde witedom
in him sylfum beon soðe gefylled."

           Then the woman unfolded   195
The rightful mystery and thus declared:
"The truth I speak through the Son of the Lord,
Savior of spirits, that I still have not
Known any man as husband
Ever upon earth. Rather it was granted me,   200
While young at home, that Gabriel,
Heaven's Archangel, should hail me in greeting.
He announced truthfully that on me heaven's Spirit
Would shine with His light, that I was to bear the Power of life,
The bright Son, Child great of God,   205
Resplendent Source of glory. Now I am His temple,
Built without sin; the Spirit of comfort
Came to rest in me. Therefore dismiss now
All your sore anxiety. Give eternal thanks
To the great Son of the Lord that I have become His mother,   210
Though virgin still, and you called His father
By the world's reckoning. The prophecy had
In His own person to be truly fulfilled.

E NOW COME TO THAT SECTION OF THE POEM WHICH IS THE most difficult to account for. Cook and others have given it the anomalous designation of "Passus," and Burgert considered it an interpolation. Its sources and its formal constitution are, and will probably remain, matters of scholarly conjecture. The passage is clearly a dialogue based on the iconological motif known to art historians as "The Doubting of Mary." [1] No convincing liturgical parallels have as yet been uncovered, but the scriptural locus of the scene is Matthew 1:18–21, verses which were employed as the Gospel reading for the Vigil of the Nativity:

> When His mother Mary was bethrothed to Joseph, before they came together, she was found to be with child, of the Holy Spirit. Whereupon Joseph her husband, being a just man, and unwilling to expose her to public shame, wanted to set the marriage contract aside privately. But while he thought about this, behold an angel of the Lord appeared to him in his sleep, saying: "Joseph, son of David, do not be afraid to accept Mary as your wife; for it is by the Holy Spirit that she has conceived this child."

The Child is then named, and the angel recalls the "Emmanuel" prophecy, which was the subject of the preceding section and accounts for the poet's sequence.

Long before it became a comic vehicle in the later Middle Ages, Joseph's confusion and dilemma was, however, a matter for greater curiosity than the biblical text could satisfy. In the apocryphal *Protoevangelium*, or *Book of James*, the expanded scene begins to take on something of the appearance of the Old English dialogue. In Chapter XIII Joseph's distress on finding the Virgin six-months pregnant is developed dramatically. He worries first

1. The motif is particularly common in Byzantine art, but see the Carolingian illumination, fig. 194, in C. R. Morey, *Early Christian Art* (Princeton, 1942), and p. 177.

about his own responsibility: "I received her out of the temple of the Lord my God a virgin and have not kept her safe," [2] then compares himself to the betrayed Adam, and finally accuses Mary directly. She, however, merely weeps bitterly and protests her purity and her ignorance of "whence it is come unto me." In the next chapter Joseph ponders his dilemma in a soliloquy which has left its mark on the Old English text: "If I hide her sin, I shall be found fighting against the law of the Lord: and if I manifest her unto the children of Israel, I fear lest that which is in her be the seed of an angel, and I shall be found delivering up innocent blood to the judgement of death." The problem is resolved as in the canonical Gospel, with the angelic appearance, but the dramatic situation is well established for future ages by the attention given to Joseph's very human perplexity and the surprising addition of Mary's grief and professed ignorance.

Though the *Protoevangelium* is not the direct source of the "Passus," the researches of Cook [3] have demonstrated that there was in the writings of the early Fathers a tradition of dramatic dialogues between the Virgin and Joseph (or Gabriel). Most of these show the influence of the *Protoevangelium,* and though no precise analogue has been unearthed, they require us to allow for the possibility of a homiletic source for the Old English text.[4] One sample, from a sermon on the Annunciation formerly ascribed to Augustine (XXXIX.2109), will serve to illustrate the rhetorical flavor with which the apocryphal text was embellished:

2. Montague Rhodes James, *The Apocryphal New Testament* (corr. ed. Oxford, 1955), p. 44.

3. Published in two articles: "A Remote Analogue to the Miracle Play," *JEGP, 4* (1902–03), 421–51; and "A Dramatic Tendency in the Fathers," *JEGP, 5* (1903–05), 62–64.

4. Burgert (*Dependence,* pp. 28–29) has shown that acquaintance with such readings could have been obtained at the Divine Office itself. The Rule of St. Benedict provides for readings from commentaries on the Scriptures "by the most renowned, orthodox, and Catholic Fathers." In the Homilary of Paulus Diaconus (XCV.1160–69), "two homilies are assigned to each Sunday and the Ember days of Advent, while the Christmas Office has as many as eleven." The choice of reading was dependent upon local custom and the limitations of the collection. This kind of literature formed the staple of monastic libraries, but since only a small portion of the material remains, it is impossible to determine more precisely whether a homily did exist whose phraseology corresponded to the Old English of the "Passus" as closely as that of the other divisions to the "Great Antiphons." If such a homily did exist, its most likely position on the Church Calendar, according to Burgert, would have been the Vigil of the Nativity.

> Joseph: What shall I do about this? How shall I behave? I am anxious,
> I groan, I suffer, I run, I seek good advice and I don't find any. Shall I
> speak up, or say nothing? What I shall do I simply do not know. Shall I
> reveal the adultery, or say nothing and avoid the disgrace? If I speak up,
> at least I will not be consenting to adultery, but I will be accused of
> cruelty, because I know that, according to the Book of Moses, she must
> be stoned to death. If I say nothing, I am consenting to evil, and I am
> casting my lot with adulterers. Since, therefore, it is wicked to say noth-
> ing, and it is worse to reveal the adultery, I will quietly put my wife
> away, lest I be responsible for murder.

Though the possibility of homiletic inspiration is perhaps as far as conjecture need take us, it is not entirely necessary to rule out a liturgical
source. The dramatic character of the "added O's" has already been re-
marked upon, and in the case of the *O Virgo virginum,* we have seen the
Old English poet respond to the challenge of the dramatic exchange, extending it even to the petition of the *Emmanuel* section. It is not totally
unlikely that antiphonal material was available to him which touched on
the "Doubting of Mary" episode.[5] But to appreciate fully this possibility,
one must first consider the question of the editing of this section on the
Old English text.

5. The *O Virgo virginum* is not the only instance of dramatic exchange
within the liturgy. For the Office of Lauds at Christmas, the Gregorian *Liber*
(LXXVIII.735) lists the following antiphons:

> Whom have you seen, O shepherds? Speak, tell us who is it that has
> appeared on the earth?—We have seen our Lord and Savior, who is born
> amid choirs of angels.
> With the angel was a multitude of the heavenly army, praising God,
> and saying: Glory to God in the highest; and on earth, peace to men of
> good will.
> The angel said to the shepherds: I bring you tidings of great joy, for
> this day is born to you the Savior of the world, alleluia!

In these three antiphons is developed the entire Shepherds' story, dramatically
expounded within the Divine Office. A similar depiction of the anxieties of
Joseph is not difficult to imagine. An exchange of words between Mary and
Joseph might have been followed by the speech of the Angel to Joseph: "Joseph,
fili David, noli timere accipere Mariam conjugem tuam" (Matt. 1:20), the
substance of which was then altered to suit the Virgin herself in the new
dramatic context. All of the matter relevant to the Old English text might have
been concentrated into two or three speeches in one or several antiphons, which
offered the raw material for paraphrase and expansion in the manner which
is the norm for this poem. If such were the case, the poetic mode of operation

It has never been questioned that the "Passus" is a dialogue between the Virgin and Joseph, concluding at line 195b with a speech of revelation where the speaker, Mary, is formally introduced. Of the remaining lines in this section a few can be assigned with certainty: lines 164–67a to Mary, and lines 175b–76a and 181b–95a to Joseph. All of the editors have accordingly divided lines 164–95a into four speeches beginning at line 164 for Mary, 167b for Joseph, 176b for Mary again, and 181b for Joseph again. This division of the verses creates a pattern strikingly dissimilar to those which surround it. The speeches are much shorter than those of the preceding sections, and indeed the interchange is much more rapid than is common to Germanic poetry of this era. Furthermore, this arrangement would force the first speech of Joseph to conclude with what is almost unquestionably a verse of invocation: *Eala fǣmne geong, mǣgð Maria.* Common Old English usage, as well as the pattern established by this poem, indicates that *eala* belongs at the beginning rather than at the end of an address, and the list of names and epithets which follows it confirms the impression.

An entirely different editing of the passage in question was suggested in 1898 by P. J. Cosijn,[6] and it is his arrangement which I have followed in my text. Cosijn divided the material into two speeches, each beginning with *eala,* giving lines 164–75a to Mary and 175b–95a to Joseph. A minor grammatical adjustment is required in lines 173b–75a, which would then be addressed to Joseph: either *minre* (174b) must be emended to *þinre,* or the masculine form *feasceaftne* (175a) must be changed to the feminine *feasceafte.* The second of these alternatives seems the more suitable, since Mary has just been lamenting her loss of reputation and the insults she has received. The unhappy situation has forced her to tears. Mary is equally upset, however, at the sorrowful dilemma which has befallen Joseph, his loss of face within the tribe for having broken the trust under which the Virgin was confided to him. With only one slight modification of the text,[7]

---

would be relatively uniform throughout, and the appearance of deviation, which has led critics to detach the "Passus" and even to consider it an interpolation, would be eliminated. Such uniformity is, of course, by no means indispensable to the poetic process, but since a potential antiphonal source has hitherto been neglected, the possibility of a fairly regular pattern of Latin originals deserves mention.

6. "Anglosaxonica IV," *Paul und Braunes Beiträge, 23* (1898), 109–30, esp. pp. 109–10.

7. In this context the further emendation offered by Cosijn in line 169, reading *for þy* in place of *for þe,* is both unnecessary and undesirable.

then, the verses under this arrangement assume an appearance not unlike that of the other divisions, giving the poem an impression of formal unity, which is lacking as it is now edited.[8]

Cook's objections to Cosijn's reading are, on close inspection, interpretive rather than editorial.[9] A psychological reconstruction of the dialogue is certainly fraught with perils, but it must be admitted that in this instance we have little more to go on. It is unlikely, however, that the passage was conceived with anything like the dramatic realism we find in the vernacular drama of the late fourteenth and fifteenth centuries. Liturgical formality is very apparent, particularly in the way Mary is transformed in her final speech from the grieving and bewildered wife into the radiant and illumined Mother of God. Furthermore, we cannot be sure of how far the poet might have been prompted to extend the reticence of Mary or the accusations of Joseph beyond the tradition known from the *Protoevangelium.* Nor can we know for certain how he conceived of the dramatic impetus for the scene—the "derisive gossip" [10] with which

8. A different arrangement of the verses was proposed by S. B. Hemingway, "Cynewulf's Christ, 11. 173b–176a," *MLN, 22* (1907), 62–63, in an attempt to correct this difficulty. He would assign lines 173b–75a to Mary, altering *minre* to *þinre* and taking the sentence as an interruption by the Virgin. In this way lines 175b–76a become on the part of Joseph "merely an exclamation of despair, mingled perhaps with reproach to his supposedly erring wife, for calling on God, whose laws she has broken." The speech beginning *hwæt bemurnest ðu* (176b) would then indicate Mary's failure to understand his sorrow. Although this arrangement accounts for the *eala* in line 175b, it does so in a manner foreign to the *Advent.* Furthermore, it increases the stichomythic rapidity of the dialogue, an effect undesirable to the tone and movement of the poem as a whole.

9. See pp. 97–98 of his edition. Objections 3, 5, and 6 depend entirely upon a dramatic reconstruction of the scene which admits other interpretations. Objections 1, 2, and 7 are discussed in my text and in the following notes. The fourth consideration, that the emendation of *feasceaftne* to *feasceafte* is "rather bold," seems perverse in view of the frequency of such slight errors in gender, easily explained by a scribe's mistaken idea that he is following the sense.

10. Cook, *Christ,* p. 98. There is no need to reject this notion, as does Neil D. Isaacs, "Who Says What in 'Advent Lyric VII'? (*Christ,* lines 164–213)," *PLL, 2* (1966), 162–66: "There can have been no rumors, or Joseph's whole problem would be nonexistent (as he now sees it), and the whole speech (ll. 185b–195a) pointless. Naturally he fears what people *might* say if they knew, but his course of action is designed to prevent such knowledge" (165). But gossip or rumors are not knowledge, and one might well imagine insinuating remarks concerning Mary's condition, without assuming that there had been any direct

the poet has replaced the apocryphal Joseph's simple discovery of his pregnant wife. It is possible to give psychological coherence to the dialogue as edited; Campbell has given a most ingenious and convincing reading in the introduction to his edition.[11] But much of any interpretation of this enigmatic exchange must remain highly conjectural, and I believe it is equally possible to justify "dramatically" the arrangement of Cosijn. I offer the following discussion merely in the interest of airing the case fully; either reading will suit my thesis concerning the poem's overall structure. We must not forget, however, the enormous advantage of bringing this section into formal alignment with the others, a consideration which Cook (p. 98) adduces in its favor and which would corroborate Campbell's belief in the formal unity of the sections.

Following Cosijn's arrangement, then, the first speech of Mary (164–75a) implies that she, too, has heard the gossip in which both she and Joseph are implicated. Her knowledge and grief have come suddenly (*lungre,* 167) upon her, as she hears his offer to dissolve whatever bonds of troth or affection lie between them:

> nu þu freode scealt fæste gedælan,
> alætan lufan mine.[12] (166–67a)

She concludes, almost despairingly, with a pious formula [13] that may have been intended to suggest an imposed reticence, a timidity before the awesome mystery of the burden she is concealing:

---

accusation which would have prevented Joseph's presumed solution of putting his wife away privily. Isaacs' assignment of speeches, though indecisively presented, allows for the reading presented here, with the exception of lines 183–85a, which he assigns to Mary for the reasons cited above.

11. Campbell, *Advent Lyrics,* pp. 22–25.

12. I find it difficult to accept Campbell's reading of these lines as a question. Cook's suggestion (p. 97), that "it would then be natural to interpret *nu,* 166, as 'since,' and to punctuate with a comma after *mine,*" would, however, give a plausible reading. It would merely assume an anterior statement by Joseph concerning the "separation." Cook's objection to the resulting pair of dependent clauses might be dismissed if *forðan* (169) were taken as indicating a looser sort of connection with the main clause (167b–68), such as "truly" or "indeed." See John C. Pope's discussion of the word in *The Seafarer,* "Dramatic Voices in *The Wanderer* and *The Seafarer,*" *Franciplegius: Medieval and Linguistic Studies in Honor of Francis Peabody Magoun, Jr.,* ed. Jess B. Bessinger, Jr., and Robert P. Creed (New York, 1965), pp. 164–93, esp. nn. 11 and 28.

13. This formula also occurs in *Beowulf,* as Hroðgar describes to the hero the hideous devastation wreaked by Grendel upon his court. In the face of what appears to be a nearly hopeless situation, he exclaims:

                    God eaþe mæg
gehælan hygesorge   heortan minre,
afrefran feasceaf*te*.   (173b–75a)

Once the possibility is allowed of Mary's access to the gossip and insults
against both partners, the speech makes good sense psychologically and
has the advantage of limiting her reluctance to enlighten Joseph to this
single occasion. It may be read with the pathos of one caught between the
involvement in divine activities of unspeakable grandeur and the ugliness
of common social realities.

The reply of Joseph (175b–95a) is also one of grief and perplexity,
yet full of dignity and honor. He had not accused her and is surprised at
her apparent confirmation of his misgivings:

                    Ne ic culpan in þe,
incan ænigne,   æfre onfunde,
womma geworhtra; [14]   ond þu þa word spricest
swa þu sylfa sie   synna gehwylcre
firena gefylled.   (177b–81a)

He, too, has begun to despair. To hear Mary speak as if she were actually
tainted by the equivocal situation in which she finds herself is almost more
than he can bear. He has had too much unhappiness over this childbearing. He accuses her no further than to confess his ignorance of what has
brought about the apparent change in her virginal condition. His dilemma
is that he is unable to give her up to a trial of which the outcome would be
death by stoning, yet to remain silent is equally a crime on his part against
the laws of his tribe:

                    Me nawþer deag,
secge ne swige.   Gif ic soð sprece,
þonne sceal Dauides   dohtor sweltan,
stanum astyrfed.   Gen strengre is
þæt ic morþor hele: scyle manswara

_____

                              God eaþe mæg
þone dolsceaðan   dæde getwæfan.   (478b–79)

The phrase seems to express almost as little faith as the modern saying, "God
only knows"—a distant pious hope in the midst of great affliction. See also
Andreas, 425b–26.

14. These phrases are better taken in reference to the Virgin than to Joseph.
There is a distinct echo of the traditional imagery of the Song of Songs—e. g.
"macula non est in te" (4:7).

laþ leoda gehwam   lifgan siþþan,
fracoð in folcum.   (189b–95a)

With these echoes of the tradition of the apocryphal legend and pseudo-Augustinian sermon, we are on familiar ground. Indeed, the sequence of ideas in the speech as a whole is perfectly logical. It has, furthermore, the great advantage, first, of beginning with an *eala* invocation, a necessary cue for the audience (or reader) to a new speaker, and second, of avoiding the shift within line 181, which would be well nigh impossible to recognize without the aid of modern punctuation. This arrangement of the speeches does more than make them formally akin to the remainder of the poem by increasing the bulk of each utterance; it also creates a tonal difference. By removing the sudden shifts of speaker, it eliminates the unpleasant querulousness which inevitably enters into a reading of the quick exchange, and lends to the personae a weight and dignity which is consonant with the occasion and the tone of the *Advent* as a whole. A more immediate advantage is that it lessens the shock of the "revelation" with which the section concludes.

The Virgin's explanation of the mystery is formally analogous to the conclusion of the *Virgo virginum* section. It is set apart by a narrative introduction and is addressed to an immediate audience of bewildered participants. Joseph now takes his place among those witnesses to the Advent who, throughout the poem, give voice to their weak understanding, their grief, and their expectation. He is a "citizen" of Jerusalem in his perplexity, and as Greenfield has suggested, his "sorrows verge on and merge with those of a spiritual exile's" (p. 328). But his relation to the historical Advent is recognizably different from those who await the Harrowing of Hell. As Mary triumphantly proclaims herself the mother of the *meotodes sunu,* she comforts Joseph with the knowledge that he shall be called His father *woruldcund bi wene* (212a). With the conclusion of this most dramatic section of the poem, we are brought into intimate contact with the historical reality of the Annunciation and move perceptibly closer to the Birth itself.

This change in the relation to the historical event is noticeable in the typology of the section as well. Though the mode here is overpoweringly dramatic, Mary in her final speech picks up Joseph's allusion to the Temple:

Nu ic his tempel eam
gefremed butan facne;   in me frofre gæst
geeardode.   (206b–08a)

The "Temple of the Lord," one of the most familiar types of the Virgin, reposes primarily upon two facts: that the Temple was consecrated and that it was constructed to contain the Ark of the Covenant. In the Second Book of Chronicles, Solomon offers a great sacrifice before the Ark, after which it is conveyed by the priest and deposited in the Temple, "in the holy of holies under the wings of the cherubim" (5:7). This ceremony completed, a great hymn of praise is sung and the Temple is filled with a mighty cloud: "For the glory of the Lord had filled the house of God" (5:14). The figure of the "corporale Dei templum" was a favorite with St. Ambrose, who, on one occasion (XVI.313), connected it with the "Emmanuel" prophecy: "From heaven, not earth, Christ chose the vessel through which He might descend, and so consecrated the temple of virginity." Elsewhere (XV. 1555), using language familiar to our poet, Ambrose calls the "temple of the Holy Spirit" a "womb of [sacred] mystery." Indeed, the figure has unusual currency among the Fathers, in sermons, treatises, and hymns. Among the Anglo-Saxons, Ælfric (*1*.546) translates the image into words which remind us of the *Advent:* "Eala ðu, eadige Godes cennestre, symle mæden Maria, tempel ðæs Halgan Gastes." When Mary employs the figure of herself in the poem, however, it has greater resonance. We recall the great architectural images with which the fragment began, the "cornerstone" and "famous hall," and then, later, the "celestial Jerusalem" itself. But here the imaginative coherence, though telling, is superficial. The "Temple" image echoes those earlier types only in its external, figurative aspect; the emphasis is profoundly different—not the active Power of the almighty Lord Himself but the earthly vessel chosen to accomplish His Incarnation. Thus the typological emphasis is subdued in both its symbolic referent and its position in the structure of the unit, while the dramatic mode is given full force and the two in consort move us closer to the longed-for event.

With the conclusion of the "Passus" section there is the sense again of another major "movement" coming to its close. We began with the lofty figures and theology of the *Oriens* division. The "light" motif of that section is now recapitulated briefly in the reference to Gabriel,[15] who

> sægde soðlice   þæt me swegles gæst
> leoman onlyhte,   sceolde ic lifes þrym
> geberan, beorhtne sunu,   bearn eacen godes,
> torhtes tirfruma*n*.   (203–06a)

Then followed the *Emmanuel* section, which provided a modal transition to the dramatic "Passus," giving immediacy to the plight as well as the

15. Cook (*Christ,* p. 99) reminds us that the reference is to Luke 1:35.

words of the ancient Prophets. Now the "movement" ends with a simple assertion of the fulfillment of prophecy:

> Sceolde witedom
> in him sylfum beon   soðe gefylled.   (212b–13)

There can be no question that this emotional confrontation of Joseph and Mary, despite its editorial problems, is an integral part of the structure of the *Advent* sequence.

Division VIII

VIII. Eala þu soða ond þu sibsuma
ealra cyninga cyning, Crist ælmihtig,   215
hu þu ær wære eallum geworden
worulde þrymmum mid þinne wuldorfæder,
cild acenned þurh his cræft ond meaht!
Nis ænig nu eorl under lyfte,
secg searoþoncol, to þæs swiðe gleaw   220
þe þæt asecgan mæge sundbuendum,
areccan mid ryhte, hu þe rodera weard
æt frymðe genom him to freobearne.
Þæt wæs þara þinga þe her þeoda cynn
gefrugnen mid folcum æt fruman ærest   225
geworden under wolcnum, þæt witig god,
lifes ordfruma, leoht ond þystro
gedælde dryhtlice, ond him wæs domes geweald.
Ond þa wisan abead weoroda ealdor:
"Nu sie geworden forþ a to widan feore   230
leoht, lixende gefea, lifgendra gehwam
þe in cneorissum cende weorðen."
Ond þa sona gelomp, þa hit swa sceolde,
leoma leohtade leoda mægþum,
torht mid tunglum, æfterþon tida bigong.   235
Sylfa sette þæt þu sunu wære
efeneardigende mid þinne engan frean
ærþon oht þisses æfre gewurde.
    Þu eart seo snyttro þe þas sidan gesceaft
mid þi waldende worhtes ealle.   240
Forþon nis ænig þæs horsc, ne þæs hygecræftig,
þe þin fromcyn mæge fira bearnum
sweotule geseþan. Cum, nu, sigores weard,
meotod moncynnes, ond þine miltse her
arfæst ywe! Us is eallum neod   245
þæt we þin medrencynn motan cunnan,
ryhtgeryno, nu we areccan ne mægon
þæt fædrencynn fier owihte.
Þu þisne middangeard milde geblissa
þurh ðinne hercyme, hælende Crist,   250
ond þa gyldnan geatu, þe in geardagum
ful longe ær bilocen stodan,
heofona heahfrea, hat ontynan,

VIII. You, O true and You, O peaceable
King of all kings, almighty Christ,   215
Before all the splendors of this worldly estate
You had being with Your glorious Father,
A Child begotten by His craft and might.
There is not now any man under the sky,
None so shrewd or sufficiently wise   220
Who might say to the people or correctly interpret,
How the Guardian of heaven at the beginning
Took to Himself a noble Son.
There came about, first of those things that human kind
Might have heard tell here among nations,   225
That at the beginning beneath the skies, sapient God,
Beginner of life, divided in a lordly way
The light from the darkness, and His was the power to decree.
And the Ruler of hosts then declared His purpose:
"Let there be now and forever forth   230
Light, a shining joy to all living things
That in generations may come to be born."
And instantly it happened, when thus it was willed,
A radiance lighted the races of man,
Bright among the stars, in the circuit of seasons.   235
Himself He ordained that You, the Son, be
Cohabitant with Your only Lord,
Before any of this ever took place.
    You are the Wisdom Who made all,
With the sovereign One, of this wide creation.   240
Wherefore there is none so enlightened or so wise,
Who may clearly trace Your lineage
To the children of men. Come now, Guardian of victory,
Maker of mankind, and manifest here
Your gracious mildness. It is needful to us all   245
That we may know Your mother's kin,
The true mysteries, since we can explain
Your paternity not one whit further.
Graciously bless this earth
Through Your coming, Christ Savior,   250
And the golden gates, which in former days
Full long ago stood locked,
High Lord of heaven, command to open,

ond usic þonne gesece þurh þin sylfes gong
eaðmod to eorþan. Us is þinra arna þearf! 255
Hafað se awyrgda wulf tostenced,
deor dædscua,° dryhten, þin eowde,
wide towrecene. Þæt ðu, waldend, ær
blode gebohtes, þæt se bealofulla
hyneð heardlice, ond him on hæft nimeð 260
ofer usse nioda lust. Forþon we, nergend, þe
biddað geornlice breostgehygdum
þæt þu hrædlice helpe gefremme
wergum wreccan, þæt se wites bona°
in helle grund hean gedreose, 265
ond þin hondgeweorc, hæleþa scyppend,
mote arisan ond on ryht cuman
to þam upcundan æþelan rice,
þonan us ær þurh synlust se swearta gæst
forteah ond fortylde, þæt we, tires wone, 270
a butan ende sculon ermþu dreogan,
butan þu usic þon ofostlicor, ece dryhten,
æt þam leodsceaþan, lifgende god,
helm alwihta, hreddan wille.

And visit us then by Your very own motion,
Humble on earth. We have need of Your mercy.   255
The malignant wolf, the beast of shadow-deeds,
Has scattered, Lord, Your flock,
Now widely dispersed. What You, Ruler, once
Bought with blood, the evil one
Oppresses fiercely, and takes in his bondage   260
Against our desires. Therefore, to You, Savior,
We eagerly pray in our innermost thoughts
That You may quickly bring help
To the weary exiles, that the tormenting murderer
To the abyss of hell may fall abject,   265
And Your handwork, Creator of mankind,
May arise and come upright
To the noble, celestial kingdom,
From which, through our sinful lust, the black spirit once
Misled and withdrew us, so that, emptied of glory,   270
Ever, unendingly, we must endure poverty,
Unless more speedily, eternal Lord,
From the enemy of man, O living God,
Protector of all beings, You will deliver us.

O Rex pacifice, Tu ante saecula nate: per auream egredere portam, re-
demptos tuos visita, et eos illuc revoca unde ruerunt per culpam.

THE OBSCURE "MONASTIC O" WHICH GOVERNS THIS SECTION MAY have been part of the liturgy for the Vigil of Christmas. Burgert (pp. 73–74) assigns it to that position on the basis of certain phrases in the antiphons still in use for Vespers of that day: "Rex pacificus" (twice) and "videbitis regem regum procedentem a matre." But the Old English poet is not concerned here with the Nativity itself or the "maternity" of Christ. Once again, as in the *Oriens* section, the poem takes a swing upward to the perspective of eternity. Taking a cue from the phrase, "Tu ante saecula nate," it returns to the high theological considerations which had also characterized the earlier passage, but the issues are viewed now from the very confines of created time. The theme once again is the eternal generation of the Son from the Father. The question of "paternity" establishes a kind of link with the ending of the "Passus," but the mode here is as distant and abstract as the preceding was immediate and dramatic.

The poet is clearly not very interested in the "pacifice" of the antiphon; he disposes of it with the *sibsuma* of the opening line and substitutes *seo snyttro* (239) as the dominant figure for this unit. Cook (p. 101) thought that there was "possibly some reference" to the "Great" *Sapientia* antiphon, with its allusions to the eternal aspect and the creative agency of the Son: "Sapientia quae ex ore altissimi prodiisti, attingens a fine usque ad finem, fortiter suaviterque disponens omnia." Burgert (pp. 30–31) dismisses the idea that the poet would have made use of so prominent an antiphon in so casual a position. The *O Sapientia* is certainly not the source of this division; more than likely, it governed the opening of the missing portion of the poetic manuscript. But it is clear that the poet is here introducing, or returning to, this great figure. The procedure is reminiscent of that in the *Clavis David* section, where the antiphonal image was given short shrift and in its stead the solar metaphor was developed—material belonging properly to the *Oriens* theme. And once again it is the imagery of light which leads the poet from the doctrine of coeternity to the figure of the "Sapientia Dei," binding his meditation still closer to the conclusion of the "Passus."

Campbell (p. 26) has pointed out how effectively the poet uses "a rhetorical pattern which virtually amounts to one of the formulae of Old English poetry" to give the feeling of "incremental emphasis" to expressions of awe and wonder before the divine mysteries. The same locution, used again and again with reference to the Virgin Birth, is here related to the Begetting of the Son. This statement—that no man is sufficiently wise that he may *areccan mid ryhte* (222a) such a marvel—takes the poet's imagining back to the origin of temporal existence. The Son "not only existed before the Creation, but he is the *Sapientia* which effected the work of creation" (p. 26).

The title of "Sapientia Dei" is assigned to the speaker of verses in the Gospel of Luke (11:49 ff). His identity is confirmed by synopsis with Matthew (23:24), where it is Christ, as Bede (XCII.486) points out, "Who calls Himself the Wisdom of God." There is, of course, ample corroboration in Old Testament texts, the most prominent being Proverbs 3:19: "The Lord by wisdom founded the earth." Of this basic tenet of Trinitarian doctrine, Rabanus Maurus (CXI. 695) offers the classical interpretation: "God the Father created all things through His Son. Figuratively, however, He founded the earth by wisdom, when, by that Son, He established the Holy Church on the firm ground of faith." A highly significant text, which the Old English poet may have had in mind, is Proverbs 8:22–30. In the *Glossa ordinaria* (CXIII.1091) the passage is associated with the prologue to the Gospel of John and was taken to refer parabolically to Christ, exhibiting His two-fold nature, human and divine. The lines are spoken by Wisdom: "The Lord possessed me in the beginning of His ways, before He had made anything at the beginning. I was established from eternity, and of old, before the earth was made. . . . When He suspended the foundations of the earth, I was with Him, forming all things." The last phrase is a very close equivalent of the Old English:

Þu eart seo snyttro   þe þas sidan gesceaft
mid þi waldende   worhtes ealle.   (239–40)

The final stamp was put on this Trinitarian figure by Augustine (XLII. 936) in his famous treatise: "The Father Himself is wisdom: and so the Son is called the Wisdom of the Father, even as He is called the Light of the Father: that is, just as light is of light and both are one light; so wisdom is understood to be of wisdom, and both are one wisdom." Augustine's analogy with the Creed gives some notion of how the complex of ideas in the *Rex pacifice* division is structured. The generation of the Son, Who became the agent of Creation, Wisdom from Wisdom and Light from Light, brings us to one of the most impressive moments of Creation, the coming of light. The poet dwells on this event in a loving digression which would be out of proportion to this section alone were the motif not one of the major structural figures of the poem as a whole. Here, in fact, the poet brings together two thematic strands which have been given considerable previous attention—the image of light and the act of Creation—both of which have been seen as manifestations of divine grace and power. The light of the Incarnation and Redemption has formerly been associated only with the Creation of man. In this division we contemplate the chief Agent of the Advent in His divine rather than His human nature, as in the preceding "Passus." We find ourselves consequently moving backward in time to the Creation of light. While the thematic significance of both passages is the same—the power of God—there is here an emphatic sense of temporal removal from the actual historical event. Indeed, one of the larger patterns observable in the *Advent* sequence shows a gradual "dramatic" approach to the historical appearance of the human nature of Christ in the holy Child, while the typological and theological sections move us continually away toward the most exalted vision of the divine nature of the Son, coeternal with the Father. This pattern of contrapuntal movement in time and in "mode of presentation" will be brought to a climax in the remaining divisions of the poem, where the theme of Creation will recur at still greater remove in eternity, while the historical event hastens toward its temporal accomplishment.

The paraphrase of the antiphonal petition in this section is ingeniously conceived. Since the true paternity of the Son is beyond human understanding, there is all the greater need *þæt we þin medrencynn motan cunnan, ryhtgeryno* (246–47a). The Virgin Birth, though mysterious, is at least a visible mystery. In any case, "to know Thy maternity" becomes simply another way of saying Thy *hercyme,* and the expression launches us into the familiar prayer for the advent of divine mercy and blessing. The allusion to the Birth is, however, accompanied by another figure of great typological interest, the "auream portam" of the antiphon, but it is inserted quite casually and its meaning has caused disagreement among the editors.

The allegory of the "closed gate" (the last in the complex of architectural figures to be introduced in the poem) is based upon Ezechiel's vision of the ideal Temple. The pertinent passage occurs at the opening of the forty-fourth chapter: "And He brought me back to the way of the gate of the outward sanctuary, which looked toward the east, and it was shut. And the Lord said to me: 'This gate shall be shut, it shall not be opened, and no man shall pass through it, because the Lord God of Israel has entered in by it, and it shall be shut.' " The figure of the "gate," as Ezechiel describes it, immediately recalls the "clavis David" and the "Oriens" [1] imagery. Traditionally, however, it was taken as a prophecy of the "physical birth of Christ," and so Cook (p. 102) [2] would read it here. Indeed, in the section which follows, the poet appears to explore at some length this concept of the figure. But at this point in the text the figure of the "gates" seems to me ambiguous, and purposely so. The usual associations with the physical birth effect a continuity with the allusion to Christ's maternity. The poet seems, however, to lean more toward a second interpretation, suggested by Dietrich [3]—the "door of heaven or paradise"—and by Campbell (p. 26), who claims that the poet "connects the closing of the gates with the expulsion from paradise." The familiar image is slipped in casually, but with an unexpected, though by no means obscure, meaning. The concept of the "heavenly gates" consorts better than the Virgin Birth, with the chief thematic concerns of this division—the splendor and power of the divine Son. It is most likely that only the gates of Paradise could be spoken of as *in geardagum ful longe ær bilocen* (251b–52); longevity is hardly to be thought of as one of the virtues of the womb of Mary. The reference is clearly to the Expulsion from Paradise, the image of locked gates recalling the "Key of David," which opened the way to some, while others were excluded. And it is to the conception of divine Judgment that the petition of this division returns, when the harried earth-dwellers request:

> þæt se wites bona
> in helle grund   hean gedreose,
> ond þin hondgeweorc,   hæleþa scyppend,
> mote arisan   ond on ryht cuman
> to þam upcundan   æþelan rice.   (264b–68)

The references to the divine power of admission and expulsion form a kind of envelope which encloses still another typological allusion, giving

1. See also Ezechiel 43:2: "Et ecce gloria Dei Israel ingrediebatur per viam orientalem."
2. See also Campbell's note, *Advent Lyrics,* p. 94.
3. See Cook's note, *Christ,* p. 102.

great figurative density to the petition. The "Good Shepherd" of John 10:11–12 is not explicitly mentioned,[4] but the rest of the parable is:

Hafað se awyrgda   wulf tostenced,
deor dædscua,   dryhten, þin eowde,
wide towrecene.   (256–58a)

This fresh image [5] for the wretched condition of man oppressed by infernal power gives a sudden, renewed intensity to the theme of "spiritual exile." The initial force of the much exploited portrait of the weary *wreccan* (264) and their captivity, *on hæft* (260), can now be recalled by means of a few slight phrases. But the passage as a whole takes on a new urgency with the increased vividness of the threat and the pathetic frailty of the sufferers in what now appears to be a desperate plight. Even the final allusion to divine Redemption comes in a conditional clause (*butan þu.* . . , 272), to which the alternative is *þæt we, tires wone, a butan ende sculon ermþu dreogan* (270b–71).

Thus the *Rex pacifice* division, like several before it, is divided between figures for the remote and awesome power of Christ and the voices of earthly petitioners for His Advent. The intensity of the plea has increased in pathos and urgency as the surrounding divisions bring us closer to the historical event. But, as in the earlier sections, the petition of the "exiles" is not confined to one set of personae, nor is it confined in time. When the poet alludes to the opening of the "golden gates," which had long stood

4. For the image of the Good Shepherd and the scattered flock, two modern French antiphons may be cited, portions of which may have been present in the liturgies of an earlier period:

O Bone Pastor, qui requiris et visitas oves: veni, et libera eas de omnibus locis in quibus dispersae fuerant in die nubis et caliginis.

O Bone Pastor, visita gregum tuum, require quod periit, reduc quod abjectum, consolida quod infirmum; ut impositas in humeros oves, in judicio pascas, et ad vitae fontes aquarum deducas.

[O Good Shepherd, You who seek and visit Your sheep: come, and deliver them from all the places to which they had been scattered in the day of cloud and darkness.

O Good Shepherd, visit Your flock, seek what has been lost, bring back what is cast down, strengthen what is weak; so that, having placed the sheep on Your shoulders, You may feed them at judgment, and lead them to the fountains of living waters.]

5. The figure itself is, of course, a commonplace. See Cook's note, *Christ*, p. 102.

closed, the reference is to the anticipation of the historical acts which began with Christ's Coming. When, a few lines later, the petitioners speak of themselves as *þæt ðu, waldend, ær blode gebohtes* (258b–59a), we are in an eternal present in which the actual Redemption has been accomplished but is in perpetual need of spiritual and liturgical renewal. Once again we are in the presence of the "double time-scheme," characteristic of those divisions in the *Advent* where the dominant theme of the eternal power of the Deity lifts the contrapuntal voices of earthbound humanity to a harmony of spiritual timelessness.

Division IX

IX. Eala þu mæra   middangeardes   275
seo clæneste   cwen ofer eorþan
þara þe gewurde   to widan feore,
hu þec mid ryhte   ealle reordberend
hata∂ ond secga∂,   hæle∂ geond foldan,
bliþe mode,   þæt þu bryd sie   280
þæs selestan   swegles bryttan.
Swylce þa hyhstan   on heofonum eac,
Cristes þegnas,   cweþa∂ ond singa∂
þæt þu sie hlæfdige   halgum meahtum
wuldorweorudes,   ond worldcundra   285
hada under heofonum,   ond helwara.
Forþon þu þæt ana   ealra monna
geþohtest þrymlice,   þristhycgende,
þæt þu þinne mæg∂had   meotude brohtes,
sealdes butan synnum.   Nan swylc ne cwom   290
ænig oþer   ofer ealle men,
bryd beaga hroden,   þe þa beorhtan lac
to heofonhame   hlutre mode
siþþan sende.   For∂on heht sigores fruma
his heahbodan   hider gefleogan   295
of his mægenþrymme   ond þe meahta sped
snude cy∂an,   þæt þu sunu dryhtnes
þurh clæne gebyrd   cennan sceolde
monnum to miltse,   ond þe, Maria, for∂
efne unwemme   a gehealdan.   300
   Eac we þæt gefrugnon,   þæt gefyrn bi þe
so∂fæst sægde   sum wo∂bora
in ealddagum,   Esaias,
þæt he wære gelæded   þæt he lifes gesteald
in þam ecan ham   eal sceawode.   305
Wlat þa swa wisfæst   witga geond þeodland
oþþæt he gestarode   þær gestaþelad wæs
æþelic ingong.   Eal wæs gebunden
deoran since   duru ormæte,
wundurclommum bewriþen.   Wende swi∂e   310
þæt ænig elda   æfre [ne]° meahte
swa fæstlice   forescyttelsas
on ecnesse   o inhebban,
oþþe ∂æs ceasterhlides   clustor onlucan,

IX. You, most renowned, O greatest on earth,   275
Throughout the world the purest queen
Of those that have been from time's beginning,
How rightly they name you, all bearers of speech,
Joyful in spirit, men in all nations,
And rightly declare that you are the bride   280
Of the most noble Prince of the sky.
So the highest in heaven, too,
The thanes of Christ, sing and declare
That you are the lady, by holy powers,
Of the glorious host, and of this world,   285
The ranks under heaven, and of hell's inhabitants,
Because you, alone of all women,
Resolved magnanimously, and with firm courage,
That you would bring to the Lord your virginity,
Offer it without sin. None like you has come,   290
None other from among all mankind thereafter,
No bride with rings adorned, who has sent
To the heavenly home with clear spirit
Such a bright gift. Therefore, the victorious Creator
Commanded His high messenger to fly this way   295
From His majestic throng, and the force of His powers
Straightway make known to you, that the Son of the Lord
In pure conception you should bring forth,
As a mercy to men, and you, Mary, henceforth
Still undefiled forever be held.   300
    We have heard further that long ago about you
A certain prophet said with authority,
In ancient days, Isaiah,
That he had been brought where he could survey
In the eternal home the whole edifice of life.   305
Then the wise sage looked beyond this land of nations
Until he perceived where was established
A noble portal. It was all bound
In precious treasure, the enormous door
Wound with strange bands. He thought surely   310
That such firm fixed bolts
None, merely human, might at any time
In all eternity ever heave open,
Or unlock the fastenings of that fortress gate,

ær him godes engel   þurh glædne geþonc   315
þa wisan onwrah   ond þæt word acwæð:
"Ic þe mæg secgan   þæt soð gewearð
þæt ðas gyldnan gatu   giet sume siþe
god sylf wile   gæstes mægne
gefælsian,   fæder ælmihtig,   320
ond þurh þa fæstan locu   foldan neosan,
ond hio þonne æfter him   ece stondað
simle singales   swa beclysed
þæt nænig oþer,   nymðe nergend god,
hy æfre ma   eft onluceð."   325
    Nu þæt is gefylled   þæt se froda þa
mid eagum þær   on wlatade.
Þu eart þæt wealldor,   þurh þe waldend frea
æne on þas eorðan   ut siðade,
ond efne swa þec gemette,   meahtum gehrodene,   330
clæne ond gecorene,   Crist ælmihtig,
swa ðe æfter him   engla þeoden
eft unmæle   ælces þinges
lioþucægan bileac,   lifes brytta.
Iowa us nu þa are   þe se engel þe,   335
godes spelboda,   Gabriel brohte.
Huru þæs biddað   burgsittende
þæt ðu þa frofre   folcum cyðe,
þinre sylfre sunu.   Siþþan we motan
anmodlice   ealle hyhtan,   340
nu we on þæt bearn foran   breostum stariað.
Geþinga us nu   þristum wordum
þæt he us ne læte   leng owihte
in þisse deaðdene   gedwolan hyran,
ac þæt he usic geferge   in fæder rice,   345
þær we sorglease   siþþan motan
wunigan in wuldre   mid weoroda god.

Until to him God's angel with gladness of mind   315
Interpreted the scene and spoke these words:
"To you I may tell what truly came about—
That some time hence the almighty Father,
God Himself, by the might of the Spirit
Will penetrate these golden gates,   320
And through these fast locks visit the earth,
And after Him then they always shall stand
Forever eternally thus closed up
That none other, but God the Savior,
May ever more unlock them again."   325
    Now that is fulfilled which the wise one then
Looked upon there with his own eyes.
You are that wall-door, through which the ruling Lord
Once journeyed out onto this earth,
And even as almighty Christ found you,   330
Adorned with virtues, pure and elect,
So after Him, the Chief of the angels,
Dispenser of life, with a key to the limbs
Closed you once more, immaculate in every way.
Show us now the grace which to you the angel,   335
God's messenger, Gabriel brought.
For this in particular earth-dwellers pray:
That you will show forth to the people that comfort,
Your own Son. Hereafter we may
All with one heart have hope,   340
Now that we look upon the Child at your breast.
Plead for us now with confident words,
That He may no longer let us obey
Error in this valley of death,
But that He may transport us to the Father's realm,   345
Where, without sorrow, thereafter we may
Dwell in glory with the God of hosts.

*O mundi Domina, regio ex semine orta, ex tuo jam Christus processit
alvo, tanquam sponsus de thalamo; hic jacet in praesepio qui et sidera regit.*

THE LAST OF THE "ADDITIONAL O'S" EMPLOYED BY OUR POET, THE
O mundi Domina was probably sung on the Eve of Christmas or
at Vespers on Christmas Day.[1] An old Italian rubric lists it
following the Gospel for the Vigil of the Nativity, the "Liber generationis,"
and preceding a solemn Te Deum. The custom of performing this antiphon
on the "Night of Mary" appears to have been widespread and may well
have been in practice in the era of the *Advent*. In any case, it is in this
section that the poet has elected to conclude the development of his historical theme and bring us to the moment of the Birth itself.

The presentation of the historical material, formerly in the dramatic
mode, here undergoes a radical change. The lofty tone of the figures in
this antiphonal invocation has led the poet to alter his strategy. The development of the thematic material is made to conform more closely to
the pattern dictated by the "Great O's." He adds a petition to the purely
descriptive and laudatory matter of the antiphon and addresses Mary
not as she was previously depicted—a historical personage involved in the
mystery of unnatural happenings—but in her most majestic state, a figure
of power, like the Christ of the "Major Antiphons":

> Eala þu mæra   middangeardes
> seo clæneste   cwen ofer eorþan
> þara þe gewurde   to widan feore.   (275–77)

This suggests the Virgin of the Coronation, not the humble girl who worried
with Joseph over appearances and gossip. To confirm this exalted vision,
the poet releases a series of impressive typological figures, only partially
indicated by the antiphon: *cwen, bryd, hlæfdige, bryd* again, and finally
wealldor. The sequence is imaginatively planned and conforms to the
highest traditions of typological ingenuity.

In a sermon on the Annunciation, printed among the spurious works of

1. See Burgert, *Dependence*, pp. 74–75; and Green, *Archaeologia, 49,* 226–
27.

St. Athanasius (*PG* XXVIII.935–40), one finds a splendid analogue for the train of associations of the Old English poet. There are three bases for the Marian epithet "Lady" or "Queen." First, she was Queen by reason of her noble birth from the loins of the great King David; she was frequently addressed, as in line 191 of our poem, as "daughter of David and Abraham." But, as she was the Mother, so she was also mystically the Bride of Him Who declared: "All power is given to me in heaven and in earth" (Matt. 28:18). And if He was the Lord God, King of all kings, then she who was crowned and took her place beside the Lord was at once "femina, Regina, Domina et Mater Dei." In this context the homilist interprets Psalm 44:10: Mary is "now like the 'queen standing on the right hand' of the King of all mankind, her own Son, and she is 'decked in the golden vestments' of incorruptibility and immortality, and 'robed in many colors.' " Furthermore, her role as "Domina" in the house of the Lord gives substance to her position as "Mediatrix," intercessor between mankind and its mighty King, thereby in effect transferring to her a portion of that power which ruled heaven and earth. "Intercede for us," the sermon concludes, "Lady and Ruler, Queen and Mother of God, for you were of our origin, and of your lineage our God was born to human flesh."

The title "Domina" or "Regina" was well observed by the Fathers and the hymnographers, particularly in moments of veneration and in prayers for intercession.[2] Her realm included, like that of her Lord, all heaven and earth, but was occasionally described as tripartite in the antique fashion. See, for example, the hymn, *Aeterne Rex altissime*[3] or the verses beginning:

Ave Dei genitrix,
coelestium,
terrestrium,
infernorum domina.[4]

Or, as Adam Scotus (CXCVIII.367) was later to refine the catalogue: "Mother of God, Queen of angels, Lover of mankind, Conqueror of devils." Thus the boundless sovereignty, received by Mary as a reward for

2. See Livius, *The Blessed Virgin,* pp. 79–81, 96, 153, 296, 298, 335, 368; Anselm Salzer, *Die Sinnbilder und Beiworte Mariens* (Linz, 1893), pp. 447–55 and, for the attribute of power over the angels, pp. 420–23; and Ippoliti Marracci, *Polyanthea Mariana* (Luca, 1710), pp. 173–86, 578–91.

3. See Cook, *Christ,* p. 104.

4. "Hail, Mother of God, Lady of heaven and earth and hell," Dreves, *Analecta, 9,* p. 62, No. 77.

her faith and obedience, increased in symbolic importance as her role in the Christian scheme of salvation expanded. The handmaiden of the Lord became Queen over all that was created.

As the pseudo-Athanasian sermon pointed out, one of the explanations for the regal epithets was the mystical conception of Mary as the "Bride of the Lord." This association of titles is obscurely implied by the phrases of the *mundi Domina* antiphon: "ex tuo jam Christus processit alvo, tanquam sponsus de thalamo." The Old English poet, however, makes the typological connections clearer, substituting "sponsa"[5] for "sponsus" and retaining the focus on Mary. In the sequence mentioned above, he moves from "queen" (275–77) to "bride" (278–81) to "lady [of the threefold kingdom]" (282–86) to "bride" again (287–94a). There is a firmness in the typological pattern here which better suits the poet's purposes than the indirection of the antiphonal figures, and the total conception is better unified. The expansion of the image lends weight to Mary's participation in the mystical espousal. She is the

> bryd beaga hroden,   þe þa beorhtan lac
> to heofonhame   hlutre mode
> . . . sende.   (292–94a)

5. "Et concupiscet rex decorem tuum: quoniam ipse est Dominus Deus tuus" are the key words of the Psalmist (44:12), which the Fathers interpreted as a reference to both the Church and the Blessed Virgin. By the mystical espousals suggested in the text, the humble maiden received the title "Domina mundi." It was, according to Chrysippus and Hesychius (Livius, *Virgin,* p. 81), a ritual in which the entire Trinity participated: "The Father will himself espouse thee for His own, the Holy Ghost will co-operate to those things which pertain to thy espousals, and the Son will assume the very beauty of thy temple." The epithalamium for these nuptials, Psalm 44, was composed by the ancestor of the holy bride, the great singer David, legendary creator of the Psalms. But in the marriage song of David's son, the Song of Songs which was Solomon's, the Fathers found ample corroboration for the Virgin's title of "Bride of Christ": "Hortus conclusus soror mea, sponsa" (4:12 and 5:1). Mary was, according to St. Ephrem (Livius, p. 383), His Mother because of His conception, His Bride because of His sanctification. In the *O mundi Domina* antiphon the mystery of the Conception is identified symbolically with the nuptial rite: "Ex tuo jam Christus processit alvo, tanquam sponsus de thalamo." A sermon of St. Proclus in praise of the God-bearer (Livius, p. 98) reflects this typological compression: "Mary is that beautiful spouse of the Canticles, who put off the old garment, washed her feet, and received the immortal Bridegroom within her own bride-chamber."

For other prefigurations of the "Mystical Marriage," see Auerbach, *Typologische Motive,* pp. 19–20.

The glamor of the occasion is given to the brilliant and deserving "bride" rather than the "emerging Bridegroom."

The gift of sinless virginity, which was Mary's nuptial offering, leads the poet to the moment of the Annunciation (294b–300), when that virtue received temporal recognition by the *sigores Fruma*. His high messenger descended from the seat of might and power to claim the bride who was to give birth to the Bridegroom, yet have her gift of virginity immaculately preserved. The subject of the Virgin Birth and the scene of angelic revelation remind the poet of a typologically related occasion, Ezechiel's vision of the "closed gate." The "thalamo" of the antiphon is economically replaced by a figure which had been ambiguously announced in the preceding division but is here accorded the most lavish visual treatment of any image in the poem. The "prophetic" passage, cited above, is here ascribed, not surprisingly, to Isaiah.[6] Twenty-five lines are devoted to a concentrated evocation of the figurative center of the vision, the heavily bolted and chained doors, and to the angelic prediction of their divine penetration. The *ceaster* (314) is referred to initially as *lifes gesteald in þam ecan ham* (304b–05a), but it is the angel's phrase, *ðas gyldnan gatu*, which brings us sharply back to the image of the *Rex pacifice* section (251–53). Ezechiel's ideal Temple is again a figure for the celestial City, but here the elaborate description is fixed at the beginning (*bi þe,* 301) and at the end (*þu eart þæt wealldor,* 328) as a type of the Virgin.

As was stated above, this explanation for the "closed gate," "porta uterus virginis Mariae" (Rabanus Maurus, CXI.385), was a commonplace from the time of the earliest Fathers of the Church and throughout the Middle Ages. Berengaud (XVII.948) [7] echoes the angel of Ezechiel in describing the "eastern gate," "which was always closed before the entry of the Prince (that is, Christ), and after his departure remained closed for all time." And Jerome (XXII.510), in an epistle, brings together a rich collection of *Advent* figures, in identifying the Virgin with the gate which was always closed and full of light, and which, closing upon itself, lets pass the Holy of Holies, the Sun of Justice, and our High Priest according to the order of Melchisedech.

The identification of the "closed door" with the "golden gates of paradise" is, of course, not a difficult one typologically. Marracci, in the *Polyanthea Mariana* (p. 130), lists innumerable epithets for the Virgin

6. See Cook's explanation, *Christ,* pp. 104–05, and Campbell's, *Advent Lyrics,* p. 96.

7. This late commentary was attributed to Ambrose, who in fact devotes the entire eighth chapter of his *De institutione virginis* (XVI.319–21) to an elaboration of this text from Ezechiel. See above, Chap. 1, p. 21.

based on the Ezechiel figure, among which are: "porta Regis," "porta Emmanuelis," "porta lucis," "porta vitae immortalis," "porta ad coelos humano generi," and "porta Paradisi." As early as the fourth century the "porta clausa" of Ezechiel was fused into a single allegory with the "golden gates of paradise." [8] Augustine [9] lends further authority to the association, and Honorius of Autun (CLXXII.905) included it in his *Speculum ecclesiae* under the feast of the Annunciation. The gate, which Ezechiel observed to be permanently closed, was that by which the King of kings passed yet left unopened: "Mary is the gate of heaven, who before, during, and after the birth, was and remained a virgin." A sermon of Alanus de Insulis (CCX.202), on the same occasion, relates that Christ entered the world to give battle to the devil, "through the golden gate with closed doors, because neither in His entrance nor in His departure was the seal of virginity broken in her." By this piece of typological linking, the "closed gate" of Mary's virginity becomes the means of opening the "golden gates of heaven." St. John Chrysostom had explained this paradox in terms of the Eve-Mary parallel: "Eve was created and the gate of paradise was closed; the Blessed Virgin was born and the Paradise of bliss was opened to all the universe." [10] And Ælfric (2.22) translated: "Ure ealde moder Eva us beleac heofenan rices geat, and seo halige Maria hit eft us geopenode, gif we hit sylfe nu mid yfelum weorcum us ne belucað."

The association of these two figures is more pertinent to the Old English poem than is at first apparent. The passage under consideration states emphatically that Ezechiel's vision is a prophecy of the Virgin Birth, and the physical equivalents are examined with an eye for physiological detail that would do justice to a "metaphysical poet":

> swa ðe æfter him   engla þeoden
> eft unmæle   ælces þinges
> lioþucægan bileac,   lifes brytta.   (332–34)

But at the close of this section of the poem we are made to recognize the importance of the alternate explanation of the figure "porta coeli." The

8. According to Epiphanius Salominus in a sermon in praise of the Blessed Virgin, the "porta coelorum" is that "of which the Prophet spoke in these words: 'Behold, the gate which is closed, etc.' " See Marracci, *Polyanthea,* p. 522.

9. Rohault de Fleury, *La Sainte Vierge, études archéologiques et iconographiques* (Paris, 1878), pp. 364–65.

10. Marracci, *Polyanthea,* p. 205.

petition (335–47), modeled on those of the "Great O's," returns us to the exalted conception of the Virgin with which the division began. Mary's role as intercessor is based, as the pseudo-Athanasian sermon attested, upon her position of "Domina" or "Regina coeli." It is from this perspective that she can be petitioned for grace and comfort, and conceded the power implied in: *Geþinga us nu þristum wordum* (342). And as the golden *wealldor* of the heavenly city, she may be asked to bring about:

> þæt he usic geferge in fæder rice,
> þær we sorglease siþþan motan
> wunigan in wuldre mid weoroda god. (345–47)

But equally, in this petition, the poet does not let us forget that the supernal role of "mediatrix" and "Domina" is founded on a temporal reality. The "grace" which the Virgin can show to mankind is that which Gabriel brought her; and the "comfort" is *þinre sylfre sunu* (339a). Her power is firmly anchored in those physical events which are brought conclusively before us in the extraordinary line:

> nu we on þæt bearn foran breostum stariað. (341)

With this simple and undramatic statement, we suddenly realize that the long-awaited Advent has been accomplished. This conclusion of what I have been calling the "historical theme" has occurred unexpectedly, not in the quasi-realistic mode of presentation of the "Passus" but in a division in which Mary has been figuratively elevated to a modal eminence formerly reserved for Christ alone. On the one hand, of course, this glorification of the Virgin is only theologically possible after the historical Birth has become a reality. On the other hand, the suppression of the dramatic excitement attendant on the physical event serves to reinforce the liturgical impact of the occasion. By this skillful adjustment of mode, the poet has conveyed the impression that the greatest moment in human time derives its magnitude only from its timelessness. At the very climax of the poem the earthly image of the Advent as a historical event is caught up and absorbed in the eternity of spiritual reality.

Division X

X. Eala þu halga   heofona dryhten,
þu mid fæder þinne   gefyrn wære
efenwesende   in þam æþelan ham.   350
Næs ænig þa giet   engel geworden,
ne þæs miclan   mægenþrymmes nan
ðe in roderum up   rice biwitigað,
þeodnes þryðgesteald   ond his þegnunga,
þa þu ærest wære   mid þone ecan frean   355
sylf settende   þas sidan gesceaft,
brade brytengrundas.   Bæm inc is gemæne
heahgæst hleofæst.   We þe, hælend Crist,
þurh eaðmedu   ealle biddað
þæt þu gehyre   hæfta stefne,   360
þinra *nied*þiowa,   nergende god,
hu we sind geswencte   þurh ure sylfra gewill.
Habbað wræcmæcgas   wergan gæstas,
hetl*an* helsceaþ*an*,°   hearde genyrwa*d*,
gebunden bealorapum.   Is seo bot gelong   365
eall æt þe anum,   ece dryhten.
Hreowcearigum help,   þæt þin hidercyme
afrefre feasceafte,   þeah we fæhþo wið þec
þurh firena lust   gefremed hæbben.
Ara nu onbehtum   ond usse yrmþa geþenc,   370
hu *we* tealtrigað   tydran mode,
hwearfiað heanlice.   Cym nu, hæleþa cyning,
ne lata to lange.   Us is lissa þearf,
þæt þu us ahredde   ond us hælogiefe
soðfæst sylle,   þæt we siþþan forð   375
þa sellan þing   symle moten
geþeon on þeode,   þinne willan.

X. O holy Lord of heaven,
You with Your Father long ago
Were coexistent in that noble home.   350
Then was no angel as yet created—
Not one of that great majestic host
Which above in the skies oversees the kingdom,
The Lord's splendid fortress, and His service—
When You at the first, with the eternal King,   355
Yourself were ordaining this wide creation,
These broad, spacious plains. Of You both together
Is the high, sheltering Spirit. Christ Savior,
To You in our lowliness we all pray
That You may hear the voice of captives,   360
Of Your forced slaves, God of deliverance—
How we are tormented through our own will.
We, outcasts, have, by the spirits of damnation,
Hostile hell-fiends, been hard constrained,
Bound with ropes of affliction. Release is dependent   365
All on You alone, eternal Lord.
Bring help to the troubled, that Your coming
May comfort the disconsolate, though against You
With sinful appetite we may have been feuding.
Have mercy on Your servants and consider our distress—   370
How we stumble with enfeebled spirit,
Abjectly go astray. Come now, King of mankind,
Do not delay too long. We have need of favor—
That You redeem us and endow us with the true
Gift of salvation, that henceforth forever   375
We may achieve here among men
That better purpose, Your will.

THE TENTH DIVISION HAS NO SINGLE AND INDISPUTABLE LITURGICAL source. The missing "Great O's," *O Radix Jesse* [1] and *O Sapientia,* [2] have been suggested, but the parallels are slight and commonplace, and, of course, the major figures are missing. Burgert's notion (pp. 37–43) that this section is an independent creation is therefore an attractive one. We have just seen how the poet was able to make over the "added" antiphon, *O mundi Domina,* on the pattern of the "Great O's." It is clearly possible, then, that here and in the next division he simply followed the antiphonal structure of the preceding divisions and supplied the material from familiar liturgical motifs. The absence, from both of these divisions, of prominent typological figures tends to suggest that the poet had exhausted the twelve "Great" and "added O's" of Advent and chose to bring his poem to a close by recapitulation rather than novelty. Burgert maintains that the poet, returning to his "favorite theme" of the coeternity of the Son with the Father, has here composed his own "O," laying "this personal tribute at the feet of Him whose Advent he had so eloquently glorified and so earnestly implored in his immortal verse." He feels, too, that the petition is "marked by an intensity of feeling and personal note seldom, if ever, equalled in any of the preceding divisions" (p.38).

The content of this division is, however, not without its liturgical con-

1. See Cook, *Christ,* p. 107.
2. See Alfred A. May, "A Source for *Christ,* 11. 348–377," *MLN, 24* (1909), 158–59. May's argument is based primarily on the idea that the second part of a verse from Ecclesiasticus (24:5): "Ego ex ore Altissimi prodivi, primogenita ante omnem creaturam," had formed the original text behind lines 348–54. The beginning of this verse was, of course, included in the *O Sapientia,* but beyond an echo of "fortiter suaviterque disponens omnia" in lines 355–57a, there is no cause for serious consideration of that antiphon as a source for this division.

nections. Burgert points out (p. 41) that the first Mass for the Feast of the Nativity has as its peculiar theme the eternal generation of the Son from the Father. We recall that the preceding antiphonal source was probably part of the Vigil of Christmas, sung at Vespers a few hours before the Midnight Mass. The Preface to that Mass elaborates the doctrine of the Begetting of Christ:

> Cujus divinae Nativitatis potentiam ingenita virtutis tuae genuit magnitudo. Quem semper Filium, et ante tempora aeterna genitum, quia tibi pleno atque perfecto aeterni Patris nomen non defuit, praedicamus, et honore, majestate atque virtute aequalem tibi cum Spiritu sancto confitemur et in trino vocabulo unicam credimus Majestatem. Et ideo cum angelis, et archangelis, cum thronis, et dominationibus, cumque omni militia coelestis exercitus, hymnum gloriae tuae canimus sine fine dicentes: . . .[3]

Here we have, as in the Old English poem, the angelic multitudes and the appearance of the Third Person of the Trinity. The latter motif points directly to the eleventh section, which is addressed to the Trinity and, like the Preface to the Mass, introduces the Sanctus.

For the petition of this section there are two prayers for the Christmas season which offer possible analogues. The theme of captivity and slavery is found in the third Mass of Christmas and in all parts of the Office for that day:

> Concede, quaesumus, omnipotens Deus: ut nos Unigeniti tui nova per carnem Nativitas liberet, quos sub peccati jugo vetusta servitas tenet.[4]

But the Ember Saturday before the last Sunday of Advent has a prayer with even more precise correspondences:

3. "The might of Whose divine Nativity was begotten by the unbegotten greatness of Your power. We declare Him always the Son and begotten before eternal time, for, in Your fullness and perfection, the name of eternal Father was not absent; and we acknowledge You equal in honor, majesty, and power with the Holy Spirit; and we believe in a single Majesty, one in three names. And therefore with Angels and Archangels, with Thrones and Dominations, and with all the militant hosts of heaven, we continuously praise Your glory in song, saying: Holy, Holy, Holy, etc."

4. "Grant, we beseech You, almighty God, that the new Birth in the flesh, of Your only begotten Son may deliver us whom the bondage of old keeps under the yoke of sin."

Deus, qui conspicis, *quia ex nostra pravitate affligimur:* concede propitius; ut *ex tua visitatione consolemur.*[5]

The first italicized phrase finds a counterpart in the line:

hu we sind geswencte   þurh ure sylfra gewill.   (362)

and the second in:

. . . þæt þin hidercyme/   afrefre feasceafte.   (367b–68a)

The closeness of these parallels ought perhaps to caution us to allow for the possibility of a lost antiphonal source for this section. As the known antiphons are composed of phrases found elsewhere in the Advent liturgy, it is not difficult to imagine one constructed from the material Burgert has provided and reflected in the Old English text:

O Rex coelorum, primogenitus ante omnem creaturam; veni ad liberandum nos, quia ex nostra pravitate affligimur; jam noli tardare.

Whether or not the source is lost or the poet is merely improvising, it is clear that he has here brought to a climax two themes which, from the beginning of our manuscript text, he has held in contrapuntal harmony. The awesome power of the Deity is again set beside the weakness and perversity of the "spiritual exiles," and each motif is accorded a conclusive statement. The coeternity of the Son and Father, as an aspect of divine majesty, has previously been the most abstract and remote way the poet has chosen to express the theme. In its previous statement the eternal distance was measured against the creation of light. Now we are removed entirely from the temporal dimension, and the divine perspective is set in relation to the first act of spiritual creation, that of the angelic hosts. Beyond this point even theology treads cautiously, and the human imagination must be content to stop at the splendid image *in þam æþelan ham* (350), where the Trinity presides over the multitudes of angels:

ðe in roderum up   rice biwitigað,
þeodnes þryðgesteald   ond his þegnunga.   (353–54)

It is this concept of angelic watch and service which unites the petition with the figurative opening of this division. In the reference to Ezechiel's

5. "God, Who see that we are afflicted by our wickedness: grant in Your mercy that we may be consoled by Your visitation."

angel and particularly in the description of Gabriel's errand in the preceding section, there have been anticipations of this theme. But now it becomes part of the structure of the unit in a new way. Unlike the angels, mankind is in a state of unhappy servitude, *gebunden bealorapum* (365a). But the images of bondage and captivity are here exposed as ominous metaphor. No longer are the "exiles" part of a historical situation where their chains and darkness may be excused as an accident of time. The blame falls squarely and repeatedly on man himself. We are afflicted *þurh ure sylfra gewill* (362), and we in humility ask for the comfort of His Coming with the full knowledge that *we fæhþo wið þec/þurh firena lust gefremed hæbben* (368b–69). But in spite of his weakness and spiritual wandering, man still recognizes that he is God's servant (*Ara nu onbehtum,* 370), and the now familiar prayer for deliverance and salvation is beautifully phrased in a request for a prevenient grace that will make his service like that of the angels, with no distinction between our will and His command:

> Us is lissa þearf,
> þæt þu us ahredde   ond us hælogiefe
> soðfæst sylle,   þæt we siþþan forð
> þa sellan þing   symle moten
> geþeon on þeode,   þinne willan.   (373b–77)

The syntax and rhythm, as well as the alliterative stress, make the final phrase a fit and natural conclusion to the thematic concerns of this division.

Enveloped in these statements of opposing will, is the final occurrence of the motif of "spiritual exile." It comes stripped of historical specificity,[6] extant now only in its timeless liturgical realm, but it comes with the full power of its antecedent figural development. Not only do the central images recur, but there are also verbal echoes of earlier movements: *wergan gæstas* (363) and *wergan heap* (16); *tydran mode* (371) and *tydran gewitt* (29); *us hælogiefe soðfæst sylle* (374b–75a) and *bring us hælolif* (150); *afrefre feasceafte* (368) and *afrefran feasceaft(n)e* (174); and particularly the line, *Is seo bot gelong eall æt þe anum* (365b–66a), which is identical to lines 152b–53a. It is a masterly touch that with this

---

6. It is perhaps worth noting that the "exile" theme, only in this final occurrence, comes close to the traditionally negative interpretation. The scriptural phrase in which the theme originates, "sedentes in tenebris et umbra mortis," is from Luke 1:79, the benediction of Zacharias, and ultimately from passages of "light and darkness" imagery in Isaiah (9:2 and 42:6,7) and Psalm 106:10: "those who sat in darkness and in the shadow of death, bound in

extensive and varied recapitulation the petitions of the exiles should come to an end, even as the theme of divine power is given its final and most unearthly statement. The counterpoint of these two motifs is here resolved. With the prayer for perfect service, the means of attaining unison is before us, and the next section will be devoted to a figuration of that ideal act of service, with man and angel united in a song to praise the most blessed Trinity.

---

want and in iron." Jerome's commentaries on Isaiah (XXIV.127) provide the standard interpretation. On the basis of Ezechiel 18:20: "the soul that sins, the same shall die," he explicates the image: "They are in the shadow of death, who although they have sinned, have not as yet left this life." His reading of Isaiah 42:7 follows a similar pattern: " 'Those sitting in the darkness out of the prison house,' are those dwelling in the night and fog of error" (XXIV.438).

Cassiodorus (LXX.769) refers the Psalmist's words to those who lived before Christ and lived in a darkness, "because they were without the light of faith and were made dark by the blindness of perfidy." They were seated, indicating the length of time they remained in that state, and the shadow of death was the "vicious life of that era, which bore the most hideous image of its future death." The chains which bound them were those of the violent death appropriate to such sinners and of the subsequent domination of the devils.

All of the later commentators subscribe to this "black" interpretation, whether in terms of those before the historical Advent or of fallen mankind in general. Our poet softens the image considerably by first referring it to those who in some way acknowledged Christ before His Coming, the Patriarchs and Prophets in limbo. Only here, in the tenth division, does he allow the concept of willful sinning to intrude, but even so, his view of man's condition is never even momentarily pessimistic.

Division XI

XI. Eala seo wlitige, weorðmynda full,
heah ond halig, heofoncund þrynes,
brade geblissad geond brytenwongas,   380
þa mid ryhte sculon reordberende,
earme eorðware, ealle mægene
hergan healice, nu us hælend god
wærfæst onwrah þæt we hine witan moton.
Forþon hy, dædhwæte, dome geswiðde,   385
þæt soðfæste seraphinnes cynn,
uppe mid englum a bremende,
unaþreotendum þrymmum singað
ful healice hludan stefne,
fægre feor ond neah. Habbaþ folgoþa   390
cyst mid cyninge. Him þæt Crist forgeaf,
þæt hy moton his ætwiste eagum brucan
simle singales, swegle gehyrste,
weorðian waldend wide ond side,
ond mid hyra fiþrum frean ælmihtges   395
onsyne wear*diað,* ecan dryhtnes,
ond ymb þeodenstol þringað georne
hwylc hyra nehst mæge ussum nergende
flihte lacan friðgeardum in.
Lofiað leoflicne ond in leohte him   400
þa word cweþað, ond wuldriað
æþelne ordfruman ealra gesceafta:
"Halig eart þu, halig, heahengla brego,
soð sigores frea, simle þu bist halig,
dryhtna dryhten! A þin dom wunað   405
eorðlic mid ældum in ælce tid
wide geweorþad. Þu eart weoroda god,
forþon þu gefyldest foldan ond rodoras,
wigendra hleo, wuldres þines,
helm alwihta. Sie þe in heannessum   410
ece hælo, ond in eorþan lof,
beorht mid beornum. Þu gebletsad leofa,
þe in dryhtnes noman dugeþum cwome
heanum to hroþre. Þe in heahþum sie
a butan ende ece herenis."   415

XI. O radiant in beauty, worshipful,
High and holy, heavenly Trinity,
Widely blessed over all the broad lands,   380
Rightly must speech-bearers, poor earthly inhabitants,
With all their power praise You highly,
Now that God the Savior, fast in His covenants,
Has disclosed to us that we may know Him.
So, too, energetically, those crowned in glory,   385
The faithful race of Seraphim
Above with the angels ever adoring,
In their unwearying multitudes sing
Most sublimely with sonorous voice,
Sweetly, far and near. They have the best   390
Of ministries with the King. To them Christ granted
That they might enjoy His presence with their very eyes
For ever and ever, and celestially clothed,
Might worship the Ruler far and wide,
And with their wings guard the face   395
Of the Lord almighty, the eternal Monarch,
And around the throne they throng eagerly,
[To see] which of them nearest our Savior
May swing in flight through the courts of peace.
They praise the Beloved, and to Him in light   400
Speak these words and glorify
The noble Author of all creation:
"Holy are You, holy, Chief of archangels,
True Prince of victory, ever You are holy,
Lord of lords; always shall Your dominion   405
Remain among earthly men in every season
Widely honored. You are the God of hosts,
For You filled the earth and the skies,
Protector of warriors, with Your glory,
Shelterer of all things. To You in the highest   410
Eternal hosanna, and on earth praise,
Bright among men. May You live blessed,
Who in the name of the Lord came to the people,
To the lowly in succor. To You on high,
Ever without end, eternal adoration."   415

OOK (P. 108) HAS LISTED TWO TRINITARIAN ANTIPHONS AS THE basis for this section. The primary source would be:

Te jure laudant, Te adorant, Te glorificant omnes creaturae tuae, O beata Trinitas.[1]

The invocation (378–80) would perhaps have been expanded under the influence of the second:

O beata et benedicta et gloriosa Trinitas, Pater et Filius et Spiritus sanctus.[2]

But this simple text is scarcely adequate to the Old English passage, although *brade geblissad* (380a) and *wlitige* (378a) may have been suggested by its "benedicta" and "gloriosa." Indeed, as Campbell (p. 31) has pointed out, neither of these sources is very helpful, because this division "is not basically a poem about the Trinity." Burgert (p. 45) has uncovered another antiphon, however, which seems better related to the whole of the *Advent* unit:

Laudemus Dominum, quem laudant Angeli, quem Cherubim et Seraphim Sanctus, Sanctus, Sanctus proclamant.[3]

The final lines of the section are, of course, a faithful and skillful paraphrase of the "Sanctus" in its entirety:

1. "All thy creatures justly praise You, worship You, glorify You, O blessed Trinity."
2. "O hallowed and blessed and glorious Trinity, Father and Son and Holy Spirit."
3. "Praise we the Lord, whom the angels praise, whom the Cherubim and Seraphim proclaim Holy, Holy, Holy." (For the Latin text, see the Gregorian *Liber,* LXXVIII. 805.)

Sanctus, Sanctus, Sanctus: Dominus Deus Sabaoth. Pleni sunt coeli et terra gloria tua. Hosanna in excelsis! Benedictus qui venit in nomine Domini. Hosanna in excelsis! [4]

This division of the *Advent* may, then, simply represent a composite by the poet of these several elements; or a single antiphon may have existed which would have combined the recognizable ingredients. In the early Middle Ages the liturgy was still in the process of development and without fixed form; antiphonaries were reproduced by hand and on occasion from memory; and authority for their use was often either arbitrary or unknown. The possibility, therefore, of a variant antiphon, now lost, is not entirely beyond conjecture. I offer the following hypothetical reconstruction for whatever interest it may have:

O beata et benedicta et gloriosa Trinitas; Te Deum trinum jure laudamus, quem laudant Angeli, quem Serephim Sanctus, Sanctus, Sanctus proclamant.

Though the source may be uncertain, the address to the Three-Person God at this point comes as no surprise. Most of the poem's major thematic material has been resolved in the preceding two sections, but simultaneously the poet has been subtly introducing this minor motif in order to bring his work to a close at the highest pitch of devotional intensity. In the tenth division the Holy Spirit was somewhat casually added to the image of the creative power of the Father and Son: *Bæm inc is gemæne heahgæst hleofæst* (357b–58a). Earlier allusions, however, have kept before us the equal participation of the three Persons in all the divine mysteries. The most notable of these occurs in the angel's speech describing the purification of the closed gates:

. . . ðas gyldnan gatu   giet sume siþe
god sylf wile   gæstes mægne
gefælsian,   fæder ælmihtig.   (318–20)

The poet is not, however, primarily interested in the theological paradoxes of the Three-in-One. He is chiefly concerned, now that his contemplation of the Advent has come to an end, with the appropriate response, the fitting service to the Deity, Who is here summoned up in His most majestic and unearthly guise. The general subject of the division is praise, and

4. "Holy, Holy, Holy, Lord God of hosts. Heaven and earth are full of thy glory. Hosanna in the highest. Blessed is he who cometh in the name of the Lord. Hosanna in the highest."

as Campbell (pp. 32–33) has demonstrated, the structure of this unit depends on the contrast between man and angel. Poor human kind, however, is no longer the main focus: the emphasis is upon the *folgoþa cyst* (390–91) of the *seraphinnes cynn,* who:

> uppe mid englum   a bremende,
> unaþreotendum   þrymmum singað
> ful healice   hludan stefne,
> fægre feor ond neah.   (387–90a)

In a superb passage of ringing sound and swift-moving flight the poet evokes the radiance of the Beatific Vision as it is known by the most exalted of angelic creatures. This is the celestial Jerusalem of which we have heard so much, seen here not as an architectural figure but as a condition of praise. The highest reward to be achieved by the greatest of His servants is:

> þæt hy motan his ætwiste   eagum brucan
> simle singales,   swegle gehyrste.   (392–93)

The relevance of this impressive scene to the Advent season has been announced in the opening lines to the Trinity:

> þa mid ryhte sculon   reordberende,
> earme eorðware,   ealle mægene
> hergan healice,   nu us hælend god
> wærfæst onwrah   þæt we hine witan moton.   (381–84)

In founding the universal Church made of living stones, in opening the way to the heavenly city, in passing through the golden gates, in making the Virgin His temple, in illuminating the world and the weary minds of men, in becoming Emmanuel, "Nobiscum-Deus," the Lord has made His earthly creatures the equal of the Seraphim and established that "Paradise within," where He may always be known. The logic of this final scene is unavoidable: when He has made Himself visible among us, there is no recourse but to unite our will with His, and this accomplished, there is nothing left but to join the angelic chorus of praise.

The Sanctus of the Mass performs liturgically precisely this function. The Christmas Preface reads: "Et ideo cum Angelis et Archangelis, cum Thronis et Dominationibus cumque omni militia coelestis exercitus, hymnum gloriae tuae canimus, sine fine dicentes: Sanctus, Sanctus, Sanctus." The Old English paraphrase reinforces the impression of angel and man singing together, providing, as Campbell (p. 33) puts it, "a synthesis of the contrast presented in the earlier sections of the poem." The parallel of "coeli et terra," *foldan ond rodoras* (408b), is enlarged in the second Hosanna to:

> Sie þe in heannessum
> ece hælo,   ond in eorþan lof,
> beorht mid beornum.   (410b–12a)

And the Benedictus is so stated that it seems to be a reference to the Advent itself:

> Þu gebletsad leofa,
> þe in dryhtnes noman   dugeþum cwome
> heanum to hroþre.   (412b–14a)

The final line returns us to our subject, eternal praise on high:

> Þe in heahþum sie
> a butan ende   ece herenis.   (414b–15)

The poem as a whole has come to rest in what is to all appearances its logical conclusion, one which is sublime yet human, like the Advent itself, in which God and man are united in one person.

Division XII

XII. Eala hwæt, þæt is wræclic wrixl   in wera life,
þætte moncynnes   milde scyppend
onfeng æt fæmnan   flæsc unwemme,
ond sio weres friga   *w*iht ne cuþe;
ne þurh sæd ne cwom   sigores agend   420
monnes ofer moldan; ac þæt wæs ma[ra]° cræft
þonne hit eorðbuend   ealle cuþan
[areccan]° þurh geryne,   hu he, rodera þrim,
heofona heahfrea,   helpe gefremede
monna cynne   þurh his modor hrif.   425
Ond swa forðgongende   folca nergend
his forgifnesse   gumum to helpe
dæleð dogra gehwam,   dryhten weoroda.
Forþon we hine domhwate   dædum ond wordum
hergen holdlice.   Þæt is healic ræd   430
monna gehwylcum   þe gemynd hafað,
þæt he symle oftost   ond inlocast
ond geornlicost   god weorþige.
He him þære lisse   lean forgildeð,
se gehalgoda   hælend sylfa,   435
efne in þam eðle   þær he ær ne cwom,
in lifgendra   londes wynne,
þær he gesælig   siþþan eardað,
ealne widan feorh   wunað butan ende.   Amen.

XII. O what a wondrous interchange in the life of man,
That mankind's mild Creator
Received from a woman flesh undefiled,
And she knew not at all a man's embrace;
Nor through seed of man upon earth   420
Came the Agent of victory; but there was a greater craft
Than all of the earth-dwellers might know
[Or reckon] in the mystery—how He, the sky's Majesty,
The high Lord of heaven, offered help
To the race of men through His mother's womb,   425
And thus going forth, the Savior of the people,
The Lord of hosts, as a help to mankind,
Confers every day His forgiveness.
For which we zealously, with deeds and words,
May praise Him devotedly. It is excellent counsel   430
To every man who has mind and memory
That he ever most often, most heartily
And most earnestly should honor God.
The sanctified [Lord,] the Savior Himself,
Will bestow upon him the reward of His favor,   435
Even in that kingdom where he never before came,
In the joy of the land of the living,
Where blessed he shall abide thereafter,
Life everlasting live without end.   Amen.

O admirabile commercium, Creator generis humani animatum corpus sumens, de Virgine nasci dignatus est: et procedens homo sine semine, largitus est nobis suam deitatem.[1]

THE ANTIPHONAL SOURCE OF THIS DIVISION, DISCOVERED BY SAMUEL Moore in 1914,[2] is a text sung during the Octave of Christmas and, in the Gregorian *Liber* (LXXVIII.741), is included specifically at Vespers of the Vigil of the Octave, the close of the celebration of the Nativity. In the *Advent* the related section functions in a somewhat similar perspective, at a considerable distance from the actual event, detached from the intense effort of contemplation and understanding and from the spiritual exaltation of the high service of praise. The poet uses this post-Advent antiphon as the foundation for a coda to the whole piece, a restrained and solemn resumé. The essential meaning of the earlier sections is epitomized: God was made man through the mystery of the Virgin Birth, but greater than this fact were the consequences of His Coming, that He brought help to all the human race and continues daily to mete out His mercy and forgiveness to errant mankind. All of this is stated with the utmost economy and hushed simplicity. All the industry and excitement of the poem has been spent with the great paean of the Sanctus of the preceding division; only the essence of the Advent remains.

The last lines of the poem return to the subject of praise. Man is advised:

þæt he symle oftost   ond inlocast
ond geornlicost   god weorþige.[3]   (432–33)

1. "O admirable interchange: the Creator of mankind, assuming a human body, deigned to be born of a Virgin: and becoming man without man's seed, bestowed on us his divinity."

2. Samuel Moore, "The Source of *Christ* 416 ff.," *MLN, 29* (1914), 226–27. Were it not for the discovery of this source and the ingenious use the poet has put it to, I would not have had the temerity to suggest and reconstruct lost antiphons for the two preceding sections.

3. The stately row of superlatives here recalls the final lines of *Beowulf* (3180–82).

The poet here has gone beyond the antiphonal source, but liturgical analogues are available. In the Gregorian Antiphonary (LXXVIII.741), when
the *O admirabile commercium* is repeated at Matins, it is followed by
verses beginning: "Quando natus es ineffabiliter ex Virgine," and concluding: "ut salvum faceres genus humanum; te laudamus, Deus noster." [4]
More relevant is perhaps the opening of the Preface of the Mass at Christ-
mastide:

> Vere dignum et justum est, aequum et salutare, nos tibi semper et ubique
> gratias agere, Domine sancte, Pater omnipotens, aeterne Deus: quia per
> incarnati Verbi mysterium, nova mentis nostrae oculis lux tuae clari-
> tatis infulsit: ut dum visibiliter Deum cognoscimus, per hunc in invisi-
> bilium amorem rapiamur. [5]

It may, however, seem unnecessary to seek a specific antecedent for a
theme which is so much a part of the liturgy in general and of the poet's
uppermost thoughts in particular, as he brings his poem to a close.

In appending this calm passage of recapitulation to his poem, so much
like a symphonic coda, the poet has used his musical ear as well as his
thematic material to give a sense of finality. The division begins with an
unusual doubling of the exclamation *Eala hwæt* in an extrametrical position, which is also extraordinary to this section. After this forceful call to
attention, what follows is sedate and measured. The sequence of thought
proceeds, plain and irrefutable, unembellished by rhetorical or typological
flourish. In the final sentence (434–39) the poet leads us once again to
an image of the eternal and celestial vision, the longed-for reward of all
those who celebrate the Advent, the focal point of all spiritual and devotional endeavor. By syntactically emphasizing the rhythmical integrity
of each line, he accomplishes, in a serene and balanced movement, what
so few Old English poets achieved, the sense of magnitude and finality be-
fitting a great literary work:

> He him þære lisse   lean forgildeð
> se gehalgoda   hælend sylfa,

4. "When you were born ineffably of the Virgin, . . . that you might save
mankind; we praise you, O our God."
5. "It is truly meet and just, right and profitable unto salvation, that we
should at all times and in all places, give thanks unto thee, O holy Lord,
Father almighty, everlasting God. For by the mystery of the Word made flesh
the light of thy glory hath shone anew upon the eyes of our mind: so that
while we acknowledge him as God seen by men, we may be drawn by him to
the love of things unseen."

efne in þam eðle   þær he ær ne cwom,
in lifgendra   londes wynne,
þær he gesælig   siþþan eardað,
ealne widan feorh   wunað butan ende.
          Amen.

4. RECAPITULATION

THE OLD ENGLISH *ADVENT* IS CLEARLY A WORK OF PENETRATING emotional and intellectual coherence. Like a large symphonic composition, it yields equally to intuitive reception and to formal analysis. But the modern reader, temporally and spiritually remote from its original audience, requires some initiation into its complex structure. In the massive detail of a comprehensive interpretation, however, the major configurations may well be obscured, and a thematic recapitulation is perhaps in order.

The *Advent* voices its argument in three predominant modes—the theological, the figurative, and the dramatic. These correspond roughly to the orchestration of a musical work and are similarly independent of the thematic content. A theme may be stated in any mode, just as a melody can be assigned to any one section of the orchestra. But whereas in music, tone or melodic coloration alone is altered, in a verbal structure, changes of an emotive character will bring with them adjustments of conceptual emphasis. The Coming of Christ, witnessed in the dramatic mode, will have a vastly different resonance from the same event presented theologically. The perspective in one case is human and historical; in the other it is supernatural and eternal. This theme, by its very nature, invites such tonal variation, for it concerns the penetration into history by the divine Agent, the reconciliation of God and man. Between these two antithetical modes of presentation lies the figurative. Drawing upon the resources of typology, it mediates between the doctrinal abstractions of the one and the concrete immediacy of the other. The liturgy, from which the antiphonal figures of the *Advent* are taken, provides a similar function. Its dramatic expression relates the spiritual consciousness of the participant to the theological absolutes which inform his condition. The *Advent* sequence, by the artful application of modal variation, acquires something of the character of a liturgical meditation.

It is clear, however, that the ordering of antiphonal material in our poem cannot have been based entirely upon liturgical usage. The intermingling of the "monastic O's" with the "Antiphonae Majores" precludes such a notion. That the poet's arrangement had a structural purpose is reflected in the modal patterns. Burgert had sensed that some of the poem's divisions fall naturally into groups. Similarly, in this commentary I have spoken of "movements," units in the poem's progress which transcend the boundaries of the antiphonal divisions. Given the fragmentary condition of the Exeter manuscript, one does not wish to insist on the regularity of such patterns. But there is an evident disjunction between sections IV and V and between VII and VIII that differs appreciably from the pause between other sections, where continuity of reference, or typological affinities, bind them together.

These divisional groupings are shaped by modal similarities. The first two "movements" conclude with sections IV and VII, the *Virgo virginum* paraphrase and the "Passus," both of which are conceived dramatically and terminate in an exalted speech by the Virgin. The sense of finality in Mary's words is increased by the confused atmosphere of apparent realism, out of which her emphatic "revelation" emerges triumphantly. The dramatic mode seems to invite a full stop. A radical shift in orientation follows. The new impetus is achieved in the *Oriens* (V) and *Rex pacifice* (VIII) divisions—as most likely it was at the lost beginning of the first unit (*Rex gentium*)—by a strong declaration in the figural mode. After the dramatic impasse of the historical perspective we begin again with the larger typological vision, under the aspect of eternity. As the poem progresses, the theological mode becomes more assertive—as it may have been in the lost opening sections—and in the final movement (VII–XI) the dramatic color has almost disappeared. The poem culminates in a hymn of praise, where again the air of finality depends, as the coda (XII) suggests, upon the contrast between the beatitude of the angelic chorus and the amazement of the terrestrial worshiper. Joining in the liturgical exercise which unites heaven and earth in harmony, the humble believer is momentarily elevated to a condition where all modal distinctions are resolved, where the theological abstraction is dramatically immediate and the figural shadow has become the present reality.

Modal coloring, or tone, is closely related to thematic statement, but the two are not to be confused. The Conception of Christ can be expressed figuratively by the image of the "Temple" or dramatically by the bewilderment of Joseph. The name "Emmanuel" is the typological form of the theological assertion of the dual nature of the Redeemer. The recurrent themes of the *Advent* are independent of any particular mode and have a direction and progression of their own. They give the poem a structure which is often synchronous with, but is not determined by, the modal "movements."

The most evident thematic sequence in the poem is that which alludes to the story of the natural event. It attracts attention by virtue of its dramatic mode, its dialogue form, and its air of controlled realism. In two short scenes, like stately mystery plays, the stark historical occasion is evoked in conspicuously human terms. The accent upon unenlightened humanity is carried to such a point that even the Blessed Virgin is, for a short while, caused to act as if she were unconscious of the mystery in which she is taking part. We are made acutely conscious of the external fact of the Advent, that not only was a Child born to Mary but that a woman, accounted a virgin, actually carried this Child in her womb, arousing the wonder and curiosity of her contemporaries and the consternation of her husband.

Because of its historical character this theme, unlike all the others, is fixed in time and has what Greenfield had hoped to find elsewhere—a chronological succession. Though one cannot be entirely certain that the missing portion of the poem did not contain some element of this sequence, the pattern as it exists has the appearance of completeness. It begins with a sudden announcement of the mystery and its central personage: *Wæs seo fæmne geong* (35b). But the magnitude of the miracle is not fully encompassed until it is contemplated first by the citizens of Jerusalem and finally by Joseph; it seems to defy both human experience and credulity. Mary's reply to the *sunu Solimæ* is quite restrained and in keeping with the inferior position of her interrogators; she reveals little of the true nature of the mystery, but promises that it brings hope of salvation to all men and women alike. Her explanation to Joseph is more inclusive, offering particulars concerning the Annunciation; yet it details only such information as is relevant to his role as earthly father of the Son of the Lord. In these two formally set speeches the interior perspective of the drama is maintained: while Mary performs like one who has been divinely touched, she revolves entirely within an earthly compass.

The chronological sequence of this historical theme is brought to a climax in the line:

nu we on þæt bearn foran   breostum stariað.   (341)

With the appearance of the Child at the breast of Mary, the Advent, in its most specific sense, is completed. The long period of the Coming is over; the Savior has arrived. It is significant, therefore, that this line is set in a division which celebrates Mary not as a participant in a human drama but as the Queen of heaven, a distant and exalted force in the Christian hierarchy. The Virgin with the Child is not an image from the Nativity scene but a fixed and symbolic power. The mystery of the Virgin Birth is now contemplated out of the historical context and in terms of an elaborate figure, the "golden gates of heaven." In accord with this modal change, the petition may now look to Mary in her supernal role of intercessor, one equipped with powers far beyond human scope. The theme has been elevated into another dimension, both the mystery and its human agents are transferred to a typological format, and the vision reaches out to eternity.

This Marian sequence, with its evident chronology and progression, functions as a backbone to the structure of the *Advent*. The Christian themes, on the other hand, are simultaneous rather than successive; they surround and give substance to the dramatic reality. The Deity and the historical personage, *mihtig meotudes bearn ond se monnes sunu* (126), are not differentiated temporally within the poem. The Child is never flesh alone: the Word of God, with all His power and wisdom, is always present. The Virgin was, of course, elevated to supernal majesty only after her terrestrial mission had been fulfilled. The creative and redemptory powers of Christ were present throughout eternity; His Advent and earthly progress alone belong to history. The differences in thematic presentation reflect this temporal distinction.

The simultaneous perspectives on the Christian themes are established quite early in the text. In the "Cornerstone" division the figures for Christ as Redeemer and Creator precede the petition that He may rescue His weary flock from its foes, as He often has in the past. The Advent here is conceived liturgically and not located, like the "mystery play" sequence, in historical time. On the other hand, in the *Clavis David* section the prayer for salvation comes from the Prophets and Patriarchs in limbo, and it is precisely the historical Advent which is anticipated, with its consequence, the Harrowing of Hell. Yet the second half of this division treats that Advent as accomplished and analyses the attendant mystery of the Virgin Birth. There is an illuminating verbal contrast within these two contiguous sections:

> Nu *sceal* liffrea
> þone wergan heap   wraþum *ahreddan* . . .   (15b–16)

> Forþon secgan mæg,   se ðe soð spriceð,
> þæt he *ahredde*,   þa forhwyrfed wæs,
> frumcyn fira.   (33–35a)

Whereas the expectant Christian looks for salvation in a hopeful future which will recapitulate the past, the pre-Christian "dweller in darkness" affirms the reality of an event which has not yet been temporally accomplished. This dual nature of the Advent furnishes the simultaneous perspective of the Christian themes throughout the poem. It is obviously another aspect of that Christian view of history, discussed in the opening section of this study, upon which the typological imagination depends. What happened at one moment in time may be extended through all history—backward in the prefigurations of the Old Testament and forward in the spiritual experience of the Church and the individual believer.

Thus, in the *Advent* poem, the "spiritual exiles," ranging from the Prophets and Patriarchs to the "metahistorical" attendant at the seasonal liturgy, participate fully in the multiple definition of the Christian themes. The audience of petitioners serves, like the typological figures themselves, to extend the temporal allusion beyond the narrow realism of the dramatic scenes. They reach out from the liturgical present to the distant shadows of Old Testament narrative, and the great figural statements of the poem are contained in an immediate yet timeless response. In fact, the Christian themes in the early portion are never without an evident reference to human affairs. As the first two "movements" proceed, this relevance is given increased prominence by a shift from the figural to the dramatic mode.

But the ordering of the figures also participates in the gradual alternation of perspective. While the opening divisions introduce the Second Person of the Trinity in His most awesome roles, as Creator, Redeemer, and Judge, the next section is devoted to Jerusalem. The multiple symbolism of that city brings the passage in line with the dual perspective of the Advent. The celestial Jerusalem, which is first invoked, is the seat of Christ in His eternal manifestation, but the earthly Jerusalem is petitioned here to prepare itself to receive the human Child. Once again the Coming is represented as both imminent and accomplished:

> Sioh . . .
> > hu þec heofones cyning
> siðe geseceð,   ond sylf *cymeð*.   (59–62)

> > Nu *is* þæt bearn *cymen,*
> awæcned to wyrpe   weorcum Ebrea.   (66b–67)

The simultaneous perspectives on the Christian theme are maintained, but the way is open for the momentary preoccupation with the Marian episode and the limited historicism of the following section.

In the next "movement" it is the literal allusion of the "Nobiscum Deus" text which gives coherence to the sequence and recalls the dual nature of the Advent. The *Oriens* passage, with its theological statement of the coeternity of the Son with the Father, seems at first to emphasize the larger perspective, but the concrete implications of the "light" image are then exploited in order to summon up the "limbo Patrum" and its prophetic view of the incarnate Redeemer. The response of the petitioners to the "Emmanuel" figure provides the transition to the dramatic mode of the "Passus."

On the whole, the *Advent* poet has minimized the importance of the historic Christ. The Marian passages present the temporally limited point of view, but the stress falls upon the human wonder and amazement before the divine mystery. For the most part, in the first half of the extant poem, the Christian themes are stated figuratively and concern the timeless functions of the Deity within time. The perspective is historical only in a larger sense. The humanly significant activities of Christ—Creation, Redemption, and Judgment—are not merely actions performed at one moment in history; they powerfully inform every moment of human experience. Equally evident in Old Testament record and in the liturgical present, they will continue to penetrate the consciousness of His creatures until the end of created time. But it is clear that the poet also conceives of God the Son as existing outside of time, and distinguishes between what might be called His metahistorical and His eternal functions. This ultimate perspective on the Christian themes is voiced primarily in the theological mode, and it is this coloration which dominates the latter half of the poem.

It is more than likely that the poem originally began on this lofty scale, with a meditation on the *Sapientia* antiphon. In the extant fragment the theme of coeternity is first expressed in the *Oriens* section. Then following the "Passus," we return to the doctrinal question of the Begetting of the Son. The first two "movements" had become progressively involved in a bewildered attempt to grasp the mystery of the Mother of God. Now the final group of sections is absorbed by the incomprehensible doctrine of divine Paternity and the attendant formulations of Trinitarian theology. So exclusive is the eternal perspective that here the Virgin, too, is perceived only in her supernal manifestation, and the final glimpse of the historical Advent is all but lost in the praise of a now timeless Mediatrix. With considerable ingenuity, a countermovement away from recorded time is further suggested by marking out the chronology of eternity. Having drawn attention to the problem of human understanding or enlightenment, the poet now breaks through the barrier of man's Creation. He asks us to contemplate the Creator Himself—now bringing forth physical illumination in the Creation of light, then giving shape to pure intelligence in the Creation of the angelic hosts. Finally, the full glory of the Trinity is realized in the allusion to Procession of the Spirit from the Father and Son. Under the awesome aspect of eternity the chorus of petitioners, now fully conscious of their sinfulness and misery, can only hope to join with the angelic orders in a "Sanctus" of praise to a Deity Whose being extends so far beyond the limits of human awareness, yet Who once dwelt among us. So, at least, the poet counsels, as he steps back from his own vision, in the simple coda which concludes his poem.

The poet of the *Advent* sequence has accomplished an extraordinary metamorphosis. With elements of a highly developed liturgy, he has restated and recreated the essence of that ritual. He has led us from distant and abstract meditation to the heart of the physical Advent, as a celebrant brings his communicants from theology to the sacrament. He has voiced our petitions and recounted our distressful condition. He has guided us beyond the historical manifestation of the mystery as far as human understanding can penetrate, then dissolved our contemplation into a triumphant hymn of praise. In conclusion, he has pointed out the way to salvation— in the words and deeds of inward devotion to the Savior. The poem itself is a paradigm of that way. The experience has been comparable to an exercise of spiritual meditation. By focusing our attention on the temporal event, the poet has in fact enlarged our vision so as to encompass the broadest significance of that moment, the magnitude of which can only lead to praise and endless devotion.

The poet of the *Advent* was obviously an artist of stature. Undoubtedly in religious orders himself, he wrote for a liturgically sophisticated audience. Skillfully he selected for his sources those antiphons which contain the essence of the Advent symbolism, and with his extensive knowledge of Christian typology, he designed a work of unusual structural imagination. His poem has not always received the attention and understanding which it merits. It must unquestionably rank among the most distinguished works in the canon of Old English poetry.

The Old English text has been supplied merely for the convenience of the reader and does not pretend to be a full scale edition. I have, therefore, severely limited textual comments to those points which affect meaning. My interpretations are, I trust, made clear in the translation, and the reader is referred to the editions mentioned in the Preface for a complete discussion of textual problems.

Italicized letters refer to obvious scribal errors and minor emendations, generally accepted by the editors. Doubtful readings are indicated by square brackets.

Lines 18–26. The text is that of J. C. Pope, Preface to the reproduction of Cook's edition, p. iv. For other suggestions see Ferdinand Holthausen, "Zum ae. *Crist I,*" *Beiblatt zur Anglia, 54* (1943), 31–32: Claes Schaar, *Critical Studies in the Cynewulf Group* (Lund, 1949), pp. 71–72; and Sherman M. Kuhn, "A Damaged Passage in the 'Exeter Book'," *JEGP, 50* (1951), 491–93.

Line 40. MS *gearnung.* Campbell (*Advent Lyrics,* pp. 84–85) attempts to justify the form as a word meaning "merit, earning." This gives a less obvious translation (though probably less satisfactory as well) than Cook's emendation, based on the arguments of Grein and Cosijn: *g[e]ea[c]nung.* The expansion of the prefix clarifies the form but is not absolutely necessary.

Line 56. *Firena* is the reading of the MS suggested by Ker in his review of the facsimile, *MÆ, 2* (1933), 226.

Line 67. Campbell translates *weorcum* as "pain, affliction," taking the form as a variant of *wærc.*

Line 69. Editors are divided on the meaning of this phrase, *niðum genedde.* I follow Klaeber, in his review of Cook, *JEGP, 4* (1902–03), 108, though the translation of *genedan* must be stretched for the occasion. *Beowulf* 2680a (and 1005a) seems, however, to be a convincing analogy. Gollancz, on the other hand, translated "He hath adventured him for men," and Cook, "He draws nigh to men."

Line 109. Campbell translates *gearo* as "of old," taking the form as a variant of *geara.*

Lines 153–54. Only an ascender (presumably of the first letter) is visible in this damaged portion of the MS. The sentence in lines 152b–53a recurs at 365b–66a, where it is followed by a vocative, but is essentially complete. It seems probable, then, that a new sentence began at 153b, and *þu for* would fill the space. (*Nu for* with a capital is possible but less likely. Schaar, p. 74, suggests *Her for.*) The verb *geseces* in 154 is a generally accepted conjecture, but the present indicative ending is fairly certain. One might translate in the future time, though the sequence of tenses is, in any reading, admittedly difficult.

Line 169. *Worde* is, according to Krapp-Dobbie (p. 249), instrumental, "in word." Most editors follow Thorpe and emend to *worda,* genetive with *worn,* "a great number of words."

Line 189. The genetive *nathwylces* after *þurh* is an anomaly, but since the meaning is clear, I have not altered the text.

Lines 206–09. Schaar (*Cynewulf Group,* p. 74) takes the *nu-nu* construction as correlative here, and Campbell follows him, translating "Now that I his temple am . . . , so you now may completely relinquish your bitter sorrow."

Line 257. Cook, following Cosijn, emends *deor dædscua* to read *deorc deaðscua,* "dark shadow of death," apparently a formula for the devil, as in *Beowulf* 160. I have retained the MS reading, with the majority of the editors, in spite of the unusual compound, since it can be appropriately translated. Campbell would add, however, a genetival ending, *-scuan,* in order to read "beast of dark deeds."

Line 264. An alternate reading of *wites bona* takes the vowel of *wites* (or emended, *wittes*) to be short. In Gollancz' translation this gives "the mind's destroyer," a kenning for the devil comparable to *gastbona,* "murderer of the spirit."

Line 311. Schaar (*Cynewulf Group,* p. 75) supports Gollancz in retaining the MS reading, without the negative: "He pondered deeply, how any mortal man might ever raise those bolts so firmly fixed, etc."

Line 364. The MS *hetlen helsceaþa* is not an impossible reading, but it involves a shift from a plural to a singular subject as well as an unlikely adjective, *hetlen,* instead of the usual *hetol.*

Lines 421, 423. The emendations are for metrical purposes. The first is Cook's, originally suggested by Sievers. The second is J. C. Pope's (see Lass, *Annuale Mediaevale, 7,* 15).

Auerbach, Erich, *Scenes from the Drama of European Literature,* New York, Meridian Books, 1959.

————*Typologische Motive in der mittelalterlichen Literatur,* Schriften und Vorträge des Petrarca-Instituts Köln, II, Krefeld, Scherpe, 1953.

Bethurum, Dorothy, ed., *Critical Approaches to Medieval Literature,* Selected Papers from the English Institute, 1958–1959, New York, Columbia University Press, 1960.

Biblia Sacra juxta Vulgatam Clementinam, Rome, Desclée, 1947.

Blake, N. F., ed., *The Phoenix,* Manchester, Manchester University Press, 1964.

Block, K. S., ed., *Ludus Coventriae, or the Plaie called Corpus Christi,* Early English Text Society, Extra Series, CXX, London, Oxford University Press, 1922.

Bosworth, Joseph, and Toller, T. Northcote, *An Anglo-Saxon Dictionary,* London, 1898.

Breviarium monasticum pro omnibus sub regula S. Patris Benedicti, 4th ed. Mechlin, 1953.

Briggs, C. A., Driver, S. R., and Plummer, A., eds., *The International Critical Commentary on the Holy Scriptures of the Old and New Testaments,* 35 vols. New York, Scribner's, 1895–1920.

Brown, Carleton, ed., *Religious Lyrics of the XIVth Century,* rev. G. V. Smithers, Oxford, Oxford University Press, 1947.

————ed., *Religious Lyrics of the XVth Century,* Oxford, Oxford University Press, 1939.

Burgert, Dom Edward, *The Dependence of Part I of Cynewulf's Christ upon the Antiphonary,* Washington, D.C., Catholic University, 1921.

Campbell, Jackson J., ed., *The Advent Lyrics of the Exeter Book,* Princeton, Princeton University Press, 1959.

Charity, A. C., *Events and Their Afterlife,* Cambridge, Cambridge University Press, 1966.

Conybeare, F. C., "The Testament of Solomon," *Jewish Quarterly Review, 11* (1899), 1–45.

Cook, Albert S., "A Dramatic Tendency in the Fathers," *JEGP, 5* (1903–05), 62–64.

———"A Remote Analogue to the Miracle Play," *JEGP, 4* (1902–03), 421–51.

———"Bemerkungen zu Cynewulfs *Christ,*" in *Philologische Studien, Festgabe für Eduard Sievers,* Halle, 1896, pp. 21–29.

———*The Christ of Cynewulf,* rev. ed. Boston, 1909. Reproduced, with a new Preface by J. C. Pope, Hamden, Conn., Archon Books, 1964.

Cosijn, Peter Jakob, "Anglosaxonica IV," *Paul und Braunes Beiträge, 23* (1898), 109–30.

Cross, J. E., "The 'Coeternal Beam' in the O. E. Advent Poem (Christ I) 11. 104–129," *Neophilologus, 48* (1964), 72–81.

Curtius, Ernst Robert, *European Literature and the Latin Middle Ages,* trans, Willard R. Trask, New York, Pantheon Books, 1953.

Daniélou, Jean, *Origen,* trans. Walter Mitchell, London and New York, Sheed and Ward, 1955.

———*Sacramentum futuri,* Paris, Beauchesne, 1950; Eng. trans. Dom Wulstan Hibberd, *From Shadows to Reality,* Westminster, Md., Newman Press, 1960.

Deimling, Hermann, ed., *The Chester Plays,* Pt. I, Early English Text Society, Extra Series, LXII, London, 1892.

Dreves, Guido Maria, *Analecta hymnica medii aevi,* 55 vols. Leipzig, 1886–1922.

Dubois, Marguerite, *Les Éléments latins dans la poésie religieuse de Cynewulf,* Paris, Droz, 1942.

Eliot, Thomas Stearns, *The Music of Poetry,* W. P. Ker Memorial Lecture, Glasgow, Jackson, 1942.

England, George, ed., *The Towneley Plays,* Early English Text Society, Extra Series, LXXI, London, 1897.

Exeter Book of Old English Poetry, with introductory chapters by R. W. Chambers, Max Förster, and Robin Flower, London, Percy Lund, 1933.

Fleury, Rohault de, *La Sainte Vierge, études archéologiques et iconographiques,* Paris, 1878.

Gardner, Helen, *The Art of T. S. Eliot,* New York, Dutton, 1950.

Gollancz, Sir Israel, ed., *The Exeter Book,* Pt. I, Early English Text Society, Original Series, CIV, London, 1895.

Goodenough, Erwin R., *By Light Light: The Mystic Gospel of Hellenistic Judaism,* New Haven, Yale University Press, 1935.

Green, Everard, "On the Words O SAPIENTIA in the Kalendar," *Archaeologia, 49* (1885), 219–41.

Greenfield, Stanley B., "Of Locks and Keys—Line 19a of the Old English *Christ*," *MLN, 67* (1952), 238–40.

——"The Theme of Spiritual Exile in *Christ I*," *PQ, 32* (1953), 321–28.

Greenhill, Eleanor Simmons, "The Child in the Tree," *Traditio, 10* (1954), 323–71.

Grein, Christian W. M., *Bibliothek der angelsächsischen Poesie,* 2 vols. Göttingen, 1857–58.

——*Sprachschatz der angel-sächsischen Dichter,* Heidelberg, Carl Winter, 1912.

Guéranger, Dom Prosper, *L'Année liturgique: L'Avent,* 13th ed. Paris, 1896.

Hemingway, Samuel B., "Cynewulf's Christ, 11. 173b–176a," *MLN, 22* (1907), 62–63.

Holthausen, Ferdinand, "Zum ae. *Crist I*," *Beiblatt zur Anglia, 54* (1943), 31–32.

Irenaeus, *Against Heresies,* trans. John Keble, London, 1872.

——*The Demonstration of the Apostolic Preaching,* trans. J. Armitage Robinson, London, S.P.C.K., 1920.

Isaacs, Neil D., "Who Says What in 'Advent Lyric VII'? (*Christ,* lines 164–213)," *PLL, 2* (1966), 162–66.

James, Montague Rhodes, *The Apocryphal New Testament,* corr. ed. Oxford, Oxford University Press, 1955.

Keil, C. F., and Delitzsch, R., eds., *Biblical Commentary on the Old Testament,* 25 vols. Edinburgh, 1857–78.

Ker, Neil R., Review of *The Exeter Book of Old English Poetry,* in *MÆ, 2* (1933), 224–31.

Klaeber, Fr., Review of Cook, *The Christ of Cynewulf,* in *JEGP, 4* (1902–03), 101–12.

Krapp, George Philip, and Dobbie, Elliott Van Kirk, eds., *The Exeter Book,* The Anglo-Saxon Poetic Records, III, New York, Columbia University Press, 1936.

Kuhn, Sherman M., "A Damaged Passage in the 'Exeter Book'," *JEGP, 50* (1951), 491–93.

Ladner, Gerhart B., "The Symbolism of the Biblical Corner Stone in the Mediaeval West," *MS, 4* (1942), 43–60.

Lampe, G. W. H., and Woollcombe, K. J., *Essays on Typology,* Studies in Biblical Theology, No. 22, London, S. C. M. Press, 1957.

Lass, Roger, "Poem as Sacrament: Transcendence of Time in the *Advent Sequence* from the Exeter Book," *Annuale Mediaevale, 7* (1966), 3–15.

Lauritis, Joseph A., Klinefelter, Ralph A., and Gallagher, Vernon F., eds., *A Critical Edition of John Lydgate's "Life of Our Lady",* Pittsburgh, Duquesne University Press, 1961.

Livius, Thomas S., *The Blessed Virgin in the Fathers of the First Six Centuries,* London, 1893.

Lubac, Henri de, *Exégèse médiévale,* 4 vols. Paris, Aubier, 1959–64.

Lundberg, Per I., *La Typologie baptismale dans l'ancienne Église,* Leipzig, Lorentz, 1942.

Lutz, J., and Perdrizet, P., eds., *Speculum humanae salvationis,* Mülhausen, Meininger, 1907–09.

MacCracken, Henry Noble, ed., *The Minor Poems of John Lydgate,* I, Early English Text Society, Extra Series, CVII, London, Oxford University Press, 1911.

McDonald, Sister Mary Francis, *Lactantius: The Minor Works,* Washington, D.C., Catholic University of America Press, 1965.

Mâle, Emile, *Religious Art in France, XIII Century,* trans. Dora Nussey, New York, Dutton, 1913.

Marracci, Ippolito, *Polyanthea Mariana,* Luca, 1710.

Marrou, Henri-Irénée, *Saint Augustin et la fin de la culture antique,* Paris, Boccard, 1938.

May, Alfred A., "A Source for *Christ,* 11. 348–377," *MLN, 24* (1909), 158–59.

Migne, J.-P., ed., *Patrologia graeca,* 161 vols. Paris, 1857–66.

———ed., *Patrologia latina,* 221 vols. Paris, 1844–64.

Milburn, R. L. P., *Early Christian Interpretations of History,* London, Black, 1954.

Miroure of Mans Salvacionne, printed privately for the Roxburghe Club, London, 1888.

Moore, Samuel, "The Source of *Christ* 416 ff.," *MLN, 29* (1914), 226–27.

Morey, C. R., *Early Christian Art,* Princeton, Princeton University Press, 1942.

Morris, Richard, ed., *Blickling Homilies,* Early English Text Society, Old Series, LVIII, LXIII, London, 1874, 1876.

Pope, John C., "Dramatic Voices in *The Wanderer* and *The Seafarer," Franciplegius: Medieval and Linguistic Studies in Honor of Francis Peabody Magoun, Jr.,* ed. Jess B. Bessinger, Jr., and Robert P. Creed, New York, New York University Press, 1965.

Richards, I. A., *Principles of Literary Criticism,* New York, Harcourt, Brace, 1959.

Robinson, F. N., ed., *The Works of Geoffrey Chaucer,* 2d ed. Cambridge, Mass., Houghton Mifflin, 1957.

Salzer, Anselm, *Die Sinnbilder und Beiworte Mariens,* Linz, 1893.

Schaar, Claes, *Critical Studies in the Cynewulf Group,* Lund, Cleerup, 1949.

Skeat, W. W., ed., *William Langland's Piers the Plowman,* London, Oxford University Press, 1924.

Smalley, Beryl, *The Study of the Bible in the Middle Ages,* Oxford, Blackwell, 1952.

Smith, A. H., "The Photography of Manuscripts," *London Mediaeval Studies, 1* (1937–39), 179–207.

Smithson, G. A., *The Old English Christian Epic,* University of California Publications in Modern Philology, I, No. 4, Berkeley, The University Press, 1910.

Stanley, E. G., ed., *Continuations and Beginnings,* London, Nelson, 1966.

Sweet, Henry, ed., *King Alfred's West-Saxon Version of Gregory's Pastoral Care,* Early English Text Society, Old Series, XLV, L, London, 1871, 1872.

Thorpe, Benjamin, ed., *Codex Exoniensis,* London, 1842.

———ed., *The Homilies of Ælfric,* 2 vols. London, 1844–46.

Toller, T. Northcote, *An Anglo-Saxon Dictionary Supplement,* Oxford, Oxford University Press, 1921.

Tuve, Rosemond, *Allegorical Imagery,* Princeton, Princeton University Press, 1966.

Wardrop, Marjory and Oliver, trans. *The Life of St. Nino,* in *Studia Biblica et Ecclesiastica,* V, No. 1, Oxford, 1900.

Wilkinson, John, *Interpretation and Community,* London, Macmillan, 1963.

Woolf, Rosemary, Review of Campbell, *The Advent Lyrics,* in *MÆ, 29* (1960), 125–29.

Wülker, Richard Paul, *Bibliothek der angelsächsischen Poesie,* 3 vols. Leipzig, 1881–98.

Wuttke, Gottfried, *Melchisedech der Priesterkönig von Salem,* Beihefte zur Zeitschrift für neutestamentliche Wissenschaft und die Kunde der älteren Kirche, V, Giessen, Töpelmann, 1927.

Young, Karl, *The Drama of the Medieval Church,* Oxford, Oxford University Press, 1933.

The patristic commentary cited in this study has been drawn from the entire medieval period. Except for the liturgical texts, these works are not offered as sources or, in most cases, as specifically influential. They are merely testimonies to the kinds of interpretation given to scriptural texts in the Middle Ages. Since we know very little about the precise material available during the eighth and ninth centuries in England, it seemed appropriate to include (tentatively) works from a much later period. Some of these later commentaries are eccentric and untraditional, but others may contain ideas of considerable antiquity not otherwise recorded or available in surviving record. As a minimal historical check, I have marked in this index by an * those authors and works known in some way during the Old English period. My authority is J. D. A. Ogilvy, *Books Known to the English 597–1066* (Cambridge, Mass., 1967), though even here the period covered extends beyond that possible for the composition of the *Advent,* and the list is necessarily far from complete.

All references are to the *Patrologiae* of Migne, still the most inclusive and generally available collection (see Ogilvy, p. i). Other individual editions and collections—especially the *Corpus scriptorum ecclesiasticorum latinorum* and *Corpus Christianorum*—have been consulted in some instances, but it was not thought necessary to include these references, given the nature of this study. Some cross-references will be found in *Clavis Patrum Latinorum,* Sacris Erudiri, III (2d ed. Brugge, 1961). Nor have I caught, I am certain, all of the false and dubious attributions in Migne's editions, especially in the homiletic collections of the great Fathers, but some of the important difficulties are cited in the notes. Where my interpretation of the poetic structure rests upon specific patristic evidence, I have tried to find some evidence of sufficient antiquity and authenticity that the ideas might have been available to the *Advent* poet.

Adam Scotus
    Sermo xxxv: In die Sanctorum Innocentium, CXCVIII.322   94
    Sermo xl: In dominica infra octavam nativitatis Domini,
    CXCVIII.367   145
Alanus de Insulis
    Elucidatio in Cantica Canticorum, CCX.94   86
    Sermo ii: In annuntiatione Beatae Mariae, CCX.202   87, 148
Alcuin *
    In Apocalypsin, C.1111   72
    1129   103
    Expositio in Epistolam Pauli Apostoli ad Hebraeos, C.1033   102
    1063   11
Amalarius *
    Liber de ordine antiphonarii, CV.1265   41 f.
    1267 ff.   44
    1268   76
    1269   92
Ambrose *
    *De Abraham admonitio,** XIV.427   13
    *Expositio evangelii secundum Lucam,** XV.1555   124
    *De fide,** XVI.607–08   13
    *De institutione virginis,** XVI.313   124
    319–21   21, 147
    *De mysteriis,** XVI.404   12,109
    Appendix: Sermo xlv: De primo Adam et secundo, XVII.692   95
Arnobius Junior *
    *In psalmos,** LIII.505   59
Athanasius *
    Expositio in psalmum lxiv, PG XXVII.283   83
    Spuria: Sermo in annuntiationem Deiparae, PG XXVIII.935–40   145
Augustine *
    *Confessiones,** XXXII.823–24   37
    *Contra Faustum,** XLII.269–70   15-16
    *Enarrationes in psalmos,** XXXVI.70, 122   84
    XXXVII.1106   83
    1493   86
    1499   64
    *De Genesi ad litteram,** XXXIV.385   108
    *Quaestiones in Heptateuchum,** XXXIV.567   12
    (*Comm. in Exod.,* 73)   623   5, 6
    *De Trinitate,** XLII.936   133
    De unitate ecclesiae, XLIII.409   84
    *Sermones dubii et spurii:**
    ii: De tentatione Abrahae a Deo, XXXVIII, 30–31   9

---

1. This work had a long history in England and Ireland before the time of King Alfred. See Dorothy Whitelock, "The Prose of Alfred's Reign," in *Continuations and Beginnings*, p. 94, esp. n. 5 for specific references. But see also, Dom G. Morin, "Le Pseudo-Bède sur les Psaumes et l'*Opus super Psalterium* de Mâitre Manegold de Lautenbach," *Revue Bénédictine*, 28 (1911), 331–40.

2. This remarkable commentary was once ascribed to St. Ambrose and is printed in Migne in the Appendix to his works, where, however, the editor designates (correctly, it would seem) the author as Berengaudus (XVII.763) on the basis of a manuscript conundrum. The identification of this writer with various ecclesiatical figures, primarily of the ninth century, rests on fragile bases, but the work can be limited on internal evidence to the ninth through twelfth centuries. See the article by E. Levesque in F. Vigoroux, *Dictionnaire de la Bible, 1*, 1610–11, and that of E. de Moreau, *Dictionnaire d'histoire et de géographie ecclésiastiques, 9*, 358–59.

3. Attributed to Walafrid Strabo in Migne, but see Dom A. Wilmart, "Un répertoire d'exégèse composé en Angleterre vers le début du XIIIᵉ siècle," *Mémorial Lagrange* (Paris, 1940), p. 339.

4. Attributed to Haymo of Halberstadt in Migne, but see H. Barré, *Les Homéliares carolingiens de l'école d'Auxerre,* Studi e Testi, **225** (1962).

5. On the authorship and probable date (twelfth century) of this collection, see Dom A. Wilmart, "Les allégories sur l'Écriture attribuées à Raban Maur," *Revue Bénédictine, 32* (1920), 47–56.

This index is limited to scriptural types, liturgical texts, and authors not included in the preceding list. Types are indicated, where possible, under proper names (e.g. "tree of Jesse" under "Jesse"). Modern works are noted by author only; further reference may be found in the *List of Works Cited*. Medieval texts are listed by author or by title if anonymous; editors are not included unless cited in my text. O-antiphons are found under their key symbols (e.g. *"O Adonai"* under *"Adonai"*), and page references include discussions of the Old English text of which the antiphon is presumed the source.